LEARN CHINESE THROUGH ENGLISH

Dr. Anita
St. Lecturer
(Department of Chinese and Japanese Studies, University of Delhi)

GOODWILL PUBLISHING HOUSE®
B-3 RATTAN JYOTI, 18 RAJENDRA PLACE
NEW DELHI -110008 (INDIA)

Published by
GOODWILL PUBLISHING HOUSE®
B-3 Rattan Jyoti, 18 Rajendra Place
New Delhi-110008 (INDIA)
Tel. : 25750801, 25820556
Fax : 91-11-25764396
E-mail : goodwillpub@vsnl.net
website : www.goodwillpublishinghouse.com

Printed at : Kumar Offset Printers, Delhi-92

PREFACE

(LEARN CHINESE THROUGH ENGLISH) is intended to be an intensive course book for beginners who have just started learning Chinese. This book lays emphasis on improving the ability of the learner to use Chinese for conversation.

In recent years, the opportunities for business and educational trips to China have increased rapidly. Without some knowledge of the Chinese language, however, you will be either confined to your hotels and offices where English is spoken or totally dependent on the sevices of an interpreter.

This book provides you the sentence pattern you will most often need and the vocabulary with which you can create new sentences. I have used not only easy-to-understand language, but also simple grammar. By recognizing the grammatical patterns each time they reappear, you will soon be able to use them on your own.

In all the chapters, the English sentence is followed by its pronunciation in Chinese, known as *pinyin* which is the official transliteration of Chinese characters. This is followed by Chinese characters, known as Hanzi. The Hanzi used in this book are the simplified characters of China. Meaning of each Chinese character is given under it in English. If you have difficulty in pronouncing a Chinese word or phrase, you can point to the accompanying Hanzi and ask the Chinese with whom you wish to communicate to read it.

In *pinyin,* I have given tones as they are listed in the dictionary. In the introduction, I have explained how tone of some words depend on the tone of the word following; so while speaking Chinese, do keep in mind this change in tones.

The key to learning a new language is repetition. Begin by practising a few simple phrases and then carry on with difficult ones.

I am very grateful to Mr. Wushan whose expertise in writing *pinyin* was a great help to me. I am very much indebted to my husband Surinder, who is also in the field Chinese language, for his valuable suggestions.

Dr. Anita

CONTENTS

INTRODUCTION

What is usually referred to as "Chinese" is really the language of the Han nationality, which makes up over 90 percent of China's population. Chinese has many dialects. ***Putonghua*** (common speech) is being popularized throughout China today. It is based on the northern dialect, with a few exceptions, with Beijing pronunciation as the standard. It is also called ***Mandarin***. The Chinese phonetic alphabet is called ***pinyin***. It is an aid to pronuncing ***putonghua***. This alphabet uses letters from the pronunciation of the Chinese characters. As the characters themselves do not represent sounds, the phonetic alphabet is a convenient tool which helps overcome difficulties in reading, writing and remembering the characters. Many of the letters have the same sound values as in Enlgish, but a few are different. Each Chinese character is one syllable which usually contains an initial and a final sound.

There are 23 initial and 36 final sounds in Chinese. Initials are all consonants, while finals are followed by a nasal consonant. De-voiced means the vocal cords do not vibrate. Palatal means the front of the tongue touches the hard palate, the front roof of the mouth. Retroflex means the tip of the tongue is slightly curled. After j, q, x, and y the two dots above ***u*** are omitted.

Key words given below in English and Hindi give only approximate sounds.

Phonetic symbols of the Chinese Language

Table of Initials

Chinese Phonetic Alphabet	English Key Words/Sounds
b	**b**ay (de-voiced)
p	**p**ay
m	**m**ay
f	**f**air
d	**d**ay (de-voiced)
t	**t**ake
n	**n**ay
l	**l**ay
g	**g**ay (de-voiced)
k	**kh**aki
h	**h**ay
j	**j**eep (palatal)
q	**ch**eese (palatal)
x	**sh**e (palatal)
zh	fu**dge** (retroflex)
ch	**ch**urch (retroflex)
sh	**sh**irt (retroflex)

r	pleasu**r**e (retroflex)
z	car**ds** (de-voiced)
c	ca**ts**
s	**s**ay
y	**y**ear
w	**w**ay

Table of Finals

Chinese Phonetic Alphabet	**English Key Words/Sounds**
a	f**a**ther
o	**o**r
e	h**e**r
i	s**ee**
i	(After c, ch, r, s, sh, z & zh, it is silent)
er	**err**
ai	**eye**
ei	sl**eigh**
ao	n**ow**
ou	**oh**
an	**ahn**
en	r**un**
ang	**ahng**

eng	h**ung**
ong	**oong**
ia	**Asia**
iao	**ee + aao**
ie	**ye**s
ian	**yen**
in	p**in**
iang	**ee + ahng**
ing	s**ing**
iong	**ee + oong**
u	r**u**de
ua	**wa**sh
uo	**wo**e
uai	**why**
uei (ui)	**way**
uan	**wan**der
uen (un)	**won**
uang	**oo + ahng**
ü	**eew / eeu**
üe	**eew + eh**
üan	**eew + an**
ün	**eew + n**

Combination Of Initials And Finals

b ba bo bai bei bao ban ben bang beng bi biao bie bian bin bing bu

p pa po pai pei pao pou pan pen pang peng pi piao pie pian pin ping pu

m ma mo me mai mei mao mou man men men men mang meng mi miao mie miu mian min ming mu

f fa fo fei fou fan fen fang feng fu

d da de dai dei dao dou dan den dang deng deng dong di diao die diu dian ding du duo dui duan dun

t ta te tai tao tou tan tang teng tong ti tiao tie tian ting tu tuo tui tuan tun

n na ne nai nei nao nou nan nen nang neng nong ni niao nie niu nian nin niang ning nu nuo nuan nü nüe

l la le lai lei lao lou lan lang leng long li lia liao lie liu lian lin liang ling lu luo luan lun lü lüe

z za ze zi zai zei zao zou zan zen zang zeng zong zu zuo zui zuan zun

c ca ce ci cai cao cou can cen cang ceng cong cu cuo cui cuan cun

s sa se si sai sao sou san sen sang seng song su suo sui suan sun

zh zha zhe zhi zhai zhei zhao zhou zhan zhen zhang zheng zhong zhu zhua zhuo zhuai zhui zhuan zhun zhuang

ch cha che chi chai chao chou chan chen chang cheng chong chu chua chuo chuai chui chuan chun chuang

sh sha she shi shai shei shao shou shan shen shang sheng shu shua shuo shuai shui shuan shun shuang

r re ri rao rou ran ren rang reng rong ru rua rou rui ruan run

j ji jia jiao jie jiu jian jin jiang jing jiong ju jue juan jun

q qi qia qiao qie qiu qian qin qiang qing qiong qu que quan qun

x xi xia xiao xie xiu xian xin xiang xing xiong xu xue xuan xun

g ga ge gai gei gao gou gan gen gang geng gong gu gua guo guai gui guan gun guang

k	ka ke kai kei kao kou kan ken kang keng kong ku kua kuo kuai kui kuan kun kuang
h	ha he hai hei hao hou han hen hang heng hong hu hua huo huai hui huan hun huang
y	yi ya yao ye you yan yin yang ying yong yu yue yuan yun
w	wu wa wo wai wei wan wang weng

These finals can be used independently as words:

a	o	e	er
ai	ei	ao	ou
an	en	ang	eng

Tones

The tone of a Chinese word is just as important as its pronunciation. This aspect of speaking Chinese is the most difficult for English speaking people to learn. In English, the tone of a word varies with the mood of the sentence; in Chinese, the tone stays the same whether the sentence is a question, exclamation or a simple statement. Mood is indicated by stress on certain words. To use a wrong tone in a Chinese word would change its meaning completely.

Chinese ***putonghua*** has four tones, expressed as 1st, 2nd, 3rd and 4th. The 1st tone (–) is a high level pitch; the 2nd tone (/) is a rising pitch; the 3rd tone (***v***) is a low dipping pitch; the 4th tone (\) is a falling tone. Even if two syllables have the same initial consonant and final, the tone may give them totally different meanings. For example:

yī	一	**one**
yí	移	**move**
yǐ	椅	**chair**
yì	译	**translate**

In addition to the four basic tones, there is one special and important change of tone called the *neutral tone*. The neutral tone is not an independent syllable that stands by itself; it occurs only in connection with and related to the tone preceding it. No tone mark is written above syllables of the neutral tone. Neutral tone is weak and short. But that does not necessarily mean that this neutral tone is less important than the other four tones, since you will never be able to speak Chinese accurately and with a natural flow if you do not know where to use a neutral tone in your speech.

The tone-mark is placed above the vowel. If there are several vowels in a word, the tone-mark is placed above the most prominent vowel (the one pronounced more loudly and clearly).

Sometimes there are changes in the tones. A few words, such as ***yī*** (one), are not always marked with the same tone when they appear in different phrases. This is because the tone of some words depends on the tone of the word following it. ***yī*** should only be spoken in the 1st tone when it stands alone or is followed by a pause; if the next word is a 1st, 2nd or 3rd tone word, ***yī*** should be read in the 4th tone ***yì***; if the next word has a 4th tone, ***yī*** should be read in the 2nd tone ***yí***. Similarly ***bù*** (not) should be read in the 4th tone only if it stands alone; ***bù*** should be pronounced in the 2nd tone ***bú*** when the word following it is a 4th tone word. For convenience, these two syllables have been marked in this book according to the tones in which they should be read within the phrase given, not as they are listed in the dictionary.

If a 1st tone is followed by a neutral tone, the 1st tone should be stressed and the next syllable should be weak and short.

If there are two similar tones, then the tone on the first syllable should be short and the tone on the second syllable should be stressed.

If a syllable of the 3rd tone is followed by a syllable of the 1st, 2nd, 4th or neutral tone, then the 3rd tone is pronounced with only the falling part of the tone without its final rise.

When a 3rd tone is followed by another 3rd tone, the first 3rd tone is read as a 2nd tone.

However, in this book we have used the original tone on the vowels so that the readers would not be confused. We hope that readers will note this while reading it aloud.

CHINESE CHARACTERS

Chinese characters are the symbols used to write Chinese. Chinese characters developed more than 3000 years ago out of ideographs. Some of these are still in use today, as for instance ***kǒu*** 口 (mouth) and ***mù*** 木 (wood). Every Chinese written character represents a one-syllable word. Many Chinese words, however, are compounds composed of two or more characters. In these compounds each character contribute a meaning to the total concept. For example, the word for film is ***diàn yǐng* (电影)**, composed of the words ***diàn*** 电 (electric) and ***yǐng*** 影 (shadow). In this book, the two syllables have been written together as one word in pinyin and two separate characters in Chinese.

Modern Chinese characters fall into two categories : one with a phonetic component, the other without it. Majority of those without a phonetic component developed from pictographs. Characters of this type which do not contain phonetic components account for only a small proportion of all Chinese characters, but many of them are in common use.

Most of the Chinese characters contain a phonetic component that tells the pronunciation and an idea component that indicates something of the meaning. For example, the idea component 口 is a picture of mouth. This component is commonly found in characters which are related to mouth such as ***chī*** 吃 (to eat) and ***hē*** 喝 (to drink). These idea components are also called radicals and are often written on the left-hand side of the character. There are more than 250 radicals.

Learning to recognize phonetics and radicals is a help to learning characters.

The phonetic component is often a character in itself. If you know the pronunciation of the character it is based on, you can know the pronunciation of many characters in which that component is used. In the word ***xià*** (吓) which means "scared", the phonetic component is ***xià*** (下), which means "early". It gives pronunciation to the character. The sound is only approximate in some characters because their pronunciation has changed over the centuries.

One of the unsolved problems of ***pinyin*** is that some characters, though written differently and with different meanings, sound the same. However, usually one can tell from the context which one to use.

Each Chinese character is composed of various strokes. These strokes are basically straight lines. From top to bottom and left to right are the main directions. There are eight basic strokes used for writing Chinese characters. These strokes are:

Dot ●

Horizontal →

Vertical ↓

Left-falling ↙

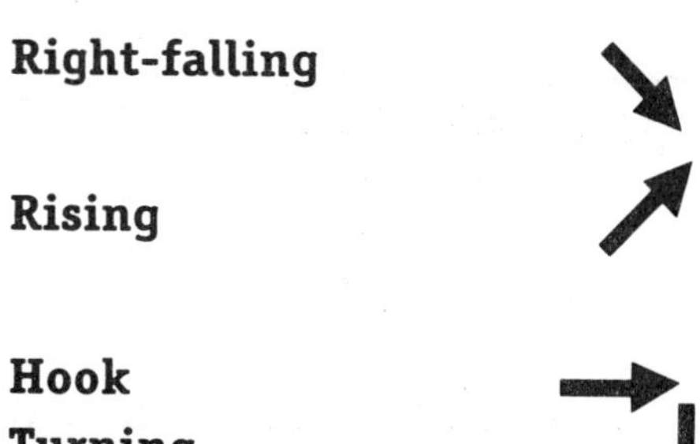

These strokes are used in a certain order to write Chinese characters. While writing characters try to follow the order of strokes given below.

1) First **horizontal**, then **vertical**.

2) First **left-falling**, then **right-falling**.

3) From **top** to **bottom**.

4) From **left** to **right**.

5) First **outside**, then **inside**.

6) Finish **inside**, then **close**.

7) **Middle**, then the **two sides**.

GRAMMAR & NOTES

Yǔ fǎ
语法

Some important grammatical patterns and notes are given in this chapter. Most of these are used in the following chapters. The easy part of learning Chinese is that there are no verb conjugations. I, you, he, we and they, all take the same verb form. For example:

I am	*Wǒ shì*	我 是
You are	*Nǐ shì*	你 是
He is	*Tā shì*	他 是
She is	*Tā shì*	她 是
We are	*Wǒmen shì*	我们 是
They are	*Tāmen shì*	他们 是
You are (pl.)	Nǐmen shì	你们 是

Plural forms are the singular forms the syllable *men*(们). Chinese nouns have no plural form. Most of the times the singular form is used after the number. For example:

One **student**	*Yī gè xué sheng*	一 个 学生
Thirty **students**	*Sān shì gè xué sheng*	三 十 个 学 生

Sentence Construction:

The basic Chinese verb sentence pattern is:

Subject + Verb + Object

Wǒ xué xi zhōng wén.
我 学习 中文。
I study Chinese.

There are phrases that describe actions such as time, place, direction and objects, they should be placed before verb. For example:

Subject + Time + Verb

Tā zǎo shang huí lai.
他 早上 回来。
He will come back in the morning.

Subject + Place + Verb

Tā cóng dà shǐ guǎn huí lái.
他 从 大使馆 回来。
He has come back from the embassy.

Subject + Object + Verb

Nǐ tí wǒ wèn hòu tā men.
你 替 我 问 候 他 们。
You convey regard to them on my behalf.

Chinese adverbs are usually placed after the subject, or before the verb and adjective. For example:

Tā gāng huí lai.
他 刚 回 来。
He has come back just now.

The sentences in which an adjective is used as the main predicate, the verb ***shì*** (是)is omitted. For example:

Zhè gè wū ze hěn gān jìng.
这 个 屋 子 很 干 净。
This room is very clean.

Wǒ de zhōng wén shū bù duō.
我 的 中 文 书 不 多。
My Chinese books are not many.

In Chinese a noun indicating time is used either before or after the subject, but never at the end of a sentence. For example:

Wǒ men xiàn zaì qù jī chǎng.
我们 现在 去 机场。
Now we go to the airport.

Xiàn zài tā qù fàn diàn.
现在 他 去 饭店。
Now he goes to the hotel.

A Chinese sentence usually contains only one active verb. But sentences with ***laí*** (来) *or* ***qù*** (去) often have two verbs, with the sentence structure like the following:

Subject + *lái / qù + Noun indicating place + Verb + Object*

Tā lái Zhōng guó xué xi zhōng wén.
他 来 中 国 学习 中 文。
He has come to China to study Chinese.

Chinese prepositions are used to introduce the time, place, direction and objects of the actions. The preposition ***zài*** (在) is used to indicate where an action takes place. The structure of a sentence with ***zài*** (在):

Subject + *zài* + Noun indicating place + Verb + Object

Wǒ zài lù shang yù dào le yī wèi péng you.
我 在 路 上 遇到 了 一位 朋 友。
I met a friend on the way.

Simple Sentences:

A simple sentence in Chinese usually consists of two parts, subject and predicate. For example:

Subject + Predicate

Yìn dù hěn dà.
印度 很 大。
India is very large.

Zhè shì dì tú.
这 是 地图。
This is a map.

In certain circumstances a subject or a predicate alone can express complete meaning. For example:

Qǐng jìn!
请 进！
Come in!

Xià yǔ le.
下 雨 了。
It is raining.

Compound Sentences:

Though subject + predicate sentences and sentences with only a subject or a predicate are two important sentence patterns in Chinese, but to express more complicated meanings, you can add words or phrases. For example:

Yuè lǎn shì lǐ bian de bào zhǐ, zá zhì hěn duō.
阅览室 里边 的 报纸 杂志 很 多。
There are many newspapers and magazines in the reading room.

Zhè shì hù zhào hé qiān zhèng.
这 是 护照 和 签证。
This is the passport and visa.

Wài guó rén tè bié xǐ huan Zhōng guó de gōng yì pǐn.
外国人 特别喜欢 中国 的 工艺品。
Foreigners like Chinese handicrafts very much.

Jīn tiān wǒ qù mín háng shòu piào chù.
今天 我 去 民航 售票处。
Today I will to the Airlines ticket counter to book a plane ticket.

Negatives:

The negative form of most verbs in Chinese is formed by adding the syllable ***bù*** (不) before the verb, almost like the word "not" in English. However, with the verb ***yǒu*** (有), the negative is formed with the syllable ***méi*** (没). For example:

Wǒ bù zhī dao.
我 不 知 道。
I do not know.

Wǒ bù míng bai
我 不 明 白。
I do not understand.

Tā bù shì dài fu , tā shì hù shi.
她 不是 大 夫，她 是 护 士。
She is not a doctor, she is a nurse.

Tā men méi yǒu lái.
他 们 没 有 来。
They have not come.

Interrogative Sentences:

Questions are formed in Chinese by adding by the syllable ***ma*** (吗) at the end of a statement or by inserting the negative form of a verb or modifier immediately after that verb or modifier. You can also make an interrogative sentence by adding interrogative pronoun in a simple sentence. For example:

Tā shì nǐ de péng you ma ?
他 是 你 的 朋 友 吗？
Is he your friend?

Nǐ néng bù néng bāng máng ?
你 能 不 能 帮 忙？
Can you help me?

Wáng Xiān sheng yǒu méi yǒu zhào xiàng jī ?
王 先 生 有 没 有 照 相 机？
Does Mr. Wang have a camera?

Nǐ shén ma shí hou huí lai ?
你 什 么 时 候 回 来？
At what time will you come back?

Nǐ shì nǎ guó rén ?
你 是 哪 国 人？
You are from which country?

Past Tense:

The past tense of a verb in Chinese is made by adding the syllable ***le*** (了) immediately after the verb or at the very end of the sentence. For example:

Wǒ qù mǎi dōng xi le.
我 去 买 东 西 了。
I went shopping.

Wǒ yǐ jīng yù dìng le yī gè fáng jiān zhù liǎng gè wǎn shang.
我已经预定 了一个 房 间 住 两 个晚 上。
I have already booked one room for two nights.

However when there is ***méi yǒu*** (没有) in the sentence, ***le*** (了) is omitted. For example:

Tā méi yǒu chī fàn.
他 没有 吃 饭。
He has not eaten.

Tā méi yǒu chū qù.
他 没有 出 去。
He has not gone out.

Future Tense:

We use ***jiāng*** (**将**) in the sentence to show future tense. For example:

Míng chén jiāng yǒu shuāng dòng.
明 晨 将 有 霜 冻。
Frost is expected tomorrow morning.

Tā míng tiān jiāng zài zhè r.
他 明 天 将 在 这 儿。
He will be here tomorrow.

Exclamatory Sentences:

Aī yā , yǔ xià de zhēn dà!
哎呀，雨 下 的 真 大！
Oh, it is really pouring!

Nà shì duō me xióng wěi de jiàn zhù a!
那 是 多 么 雄 伟 的 建 筑 啊！
How magnificent those structures are!

Use of *yī xià* (一下):

Yī xià **(一下)** indicates a very short period of time. For example:

Qǐng děng yī xià.
请 等 一下。
Please wait a moment.

Qǐng tián yī xià zhè zhāng biǎo.
请 填 一下 这 张 表。
Please fill this form.

Use of *cóng... dào...* (从....到....):

The words ***còng.... dào....*** **(从....到....)**mean "from.... to....", indicating both time and place. For example:

Cóng zhè er dào Běi jīng fàn diàn hěn jìn.
从 这儿 到 北京 饭店 很 近。
From here Beijing Hotel is very near.

Wǒ men cóng bā diǎn dào shí èr diǎn gōng zuò.
我们 从 八点 到 十二点 工 作。
We work from eight o'clock to twelve o'clock.

Use of *Bǎ* (把):

The ***bǎ*** (把) structure is a unique sentence structure in Chinese. To give emphasis to the action in the latter part of a sentence, the syllable ***bǎ*** (把) and the object of the sentence is brought forward before the verb. For example:

Qǐng bǎ zhè tiáo kù zi xǐ gān jìng.
请 把 这 条 裤子 洗 干 净。
Please wash these trousers clean.

Qǐng bǎ nà jiàn pí dà yī ná lái kàn kàn.
请 把 那 件 皮 大衣 拿 来 看 看。
Please take that fur coat for me to have a look.

The negative is formed by adding ***bù*** (不) or ***méi yǒu*** (没有) before ***bǎ*** (把). For example:

Tā méi bǎ pí dà yī gěi wǒ.
他 没 把 皮 大衣 给 我。
He did not give the fur coat to me.

Tā méi bǎ zhè tiáo kù zi xǐ gān jìng.
他 没 把 这 条 裤子 洗 干 净。
He did not wash these trousers clean.

Use of *le* (了) (to indicate a change):

One of the functions of ***le*** (了), as an auxiliary word added to the end of a sentence, is to indicate mood, the coming of new things or a change in the state of affairs. For example:

Xià yǔ le.
下 雨 了。
It is beginning to rain.

Xīng qī liù le.
星 期 六 了。
It is Saturday.

Yè zi hóng le.
叶 子 红 了。
The leaves are turning red.

Use of aspect particle *guò* (过):

The aspect particle ***guò*** (过) shows that an action did happen sometime in the past, with the stress on the fact that one has had such a past experience. For example:

Wǒ men qù guò Cháng chéng.
我 们 去 过 长 城。
We have been to the Great Wall.

In a negative sentence, ***méi yǒu*** (没 有) is used before the verb. For example:

Lái Běijīng yǐ hòu, wǒ hái méi yǒu qù guò Yí hé yuán.
来 北京以后，我还 没有 去过 颐和园。
After coming to Beijing, I still have not been to the Summer Palace.

Use of *zhe* (着) :

Zhe (着) is a suffix. When added to a verb, it can indicate the continuation of an action or a state. The negative form is ***méi*** (没) ...***zhe*** (着). For example:

Lǎo shī zhàn zhe jiǎng, xué sheng zuò zhe tīng.
老师 站 着 讲，学 生 坐 着 听。
The teacher stands to give his lecture, while the students sit to listen.

Guó jì jù lè bù bù yuǎn, cóng zhè er zǒu zhe qù
国际俱乐部 不 远，从 这儿 走 着 去
shí fēn zhōng jìu dào le.
十 分 钟 就 到 了。

The International Club is not far from here. You can get there on foot in ten minutes.

Wáng xiān sheng méi ná zhe zá zhì, tā ná zhe bào zhǐ ne!
王 先 生 没 拿着杂志，他拿着报纸呢！
Mr. Wang is holding a newspaper, not a magazine, in his hands.

Use of *lí* (离) & *cóng* (从):

The preposition ***lí*** (离) or ***cóng*** (从) take a word or phrase denoting place or time as its object. For example:

Wǒ men de fàn diàn lí dà shǐ guǎn bù yuǎn.
我们 的 饭 店 离大使馆 不 远。
Our hotel is not far from the embassy.

Shàng wǔ wǒ men cóng jiǔ diǎn kāi hui.
上 午 我们 从 九点 开 会。
We will start meeting in the morning from nine o'clock.

Use of *shì..... de* (是 . . . . 的) construction:

The ***shì.... de*** (是 . . . 的) structure is used to highlight when, where, or just how an action was accomplished. The structure is:

Subject + *shì* + Adverb indicating time/place/way + Verb + *de*

Wǒ Shì zuò fēi jī huí lai de.
我 是 坐 飞机 回来 的。
I have come back by plane.

Zhè jiàn yī fu wǒ zài Běi jīng mǎi de.
这 件 衣服 我 在 北京 买 的。
I have bought this dress in Beijing.

Comparative Sentences:

In Chinese there are two basic sentence structures used to compare one thing with another:

1) A + ***gēn*****(跟)** +B +***yī yàng*** (一样)/***bù yī yàng*** (不一样)

Tā de shū gēn wǒ de yī yàng / bù yī yàng.
他 的 书 跟 我 的 一样 / 不 一样。
His book is same / not same as mine.

2) A + ***bǐ*** / ***bù bǐ*** (比 / 不 比) + B + Adjective

Tā bǐ / bù bǐ wǒ gāo.
他 比 / 不比 我 高。
He is / is not taller than me.

However, ***bù rú*** (不 如)is used to form a negative comparison, similar to "not as.......as" in English. It is often used in the following structure:

A + ***bù rú*** (不如) + B + Adjective

Tā bù rú nǐ piào liang.
她 不如 你 漂 亮。
She is not as beautiful as you are.

Zài jiā kàn diàn shì bù rú dào qiú cháng kàn hǎo.
在 家 看 电 视 不如 到 球 场 看 好。
Watching a television game is not the same thing as watching it on the spot.

Use of *yào..... le* (要 . . . 了) structure:

The ***yào.....le*** (要 . . . . 了) is used to indicate that something is about to happen or a situation will soon occur. For example:

Fēi jī yào qǐ fēi le.
飞机 要 起飞了。
The plane is going to take off.

Yào xià xuě le.
要 下 雪 了。
It is going to snow.

Use of *De* (的) construction:

The structural particle ***De*** (得) is used to connect the attributive and what it qualifies. For example:

Shàng hǎi shì Zhōng guó zuì dà de chéng shì.
上 海 是 中 国 最 大 的 城 市。
Shanghai is the biggest city of China.

Tā men dōu shì cóng Yìn dù lái de.
他们 都 是 从 印 度 来 的。
All of them have come from India.

Use of *De* (得) structure:

De(得)is a structural particle used in front of a complement of degree. The sentence structure "Subject + Verb + *de* + Adjective" is used to express the mood or consequence of an action. For example:

Shí jiān guò de hěn kuài.
时 间 过 得 很 快。
Time passes very fast.

Tā hàn yǔ shuō de hěn hǎo.
他 汉 语 说 的 很 好。
He speaks Chinese very well.

Use of *di* (地) structure:

The structural particle ***di*(地)** is used after the adverbial adjunct to modify a verb or an adjective.

Jīn tiān xiū xi, dà jiā dōu hěn gāo xìng di qù chéng lǐ wán.
今天休息，大家都很高兴地去城里玩。
Today is a day off, everybody happily went to the city for enjoyment.

Lǎo shī wèn de wèn tí tā hěn qīng chu di huí dá le.
老师问的问题他很清楚地回答了。
He replied all the questions asked by the teacher very clearly.

Yǒu.......yòu....... (又...又) structure:

Yòu..... yòu....... (又...又) is a very commonly used structure in Chinese. With ***yòu*** (又)linking two verbs or adjectives, it may indicate two simultaneous actions or the co-existence of two situations at the same time. For example:

Yòu gāo yòu dà.
又高又大。
Tall as well as big.

You leng you gan zao.
又 冷 又 干燥。
Cold as well as dry.

Use of *jiu* (就) and *cai* (才):

The adverb ***jiu*** (就) and ***cai*** (才) are used to emphasize early or late happening of something or of an action. For example:

Wo zao shang wu dian jiu qi chuang le.
我 早 上 五点 就 起 床 了。
I got up at five o'clock.

Ta jiu dian ban cai qi chuang le.
他 九 点 半 才 起 床 了。
He got up only at half past nine.

Use of *Bei / Rang* (被 / 让) construction:

Bei / rang (被 / 让) is used to form a passive voice, usually in the following pattern:

A + *bei / rang* + B + Verb

Shu bei ta na zou le.
书 被 他 拿 走 了。
Book is taken away by him.

Wǒ ràng tā qù mǎi fēi jī piào.
我 让 他 去 买 飞机票。
I asked him to buy a plane ticket.

Use Of *Lián ... dōu* (连...都) structure:

The ***lián.... dōu*** (连...都) structure helps add strength to a surprising statement, approximating something like "even" in English. For example:

Lián xiǎo hái zi dōu zhī dao zhè ge dào li.
连 小 孩 子 都 知 道 这 个 道 理。
Even a small child knows this logic.

Wǒ lián xiǎng dōu méi yǒu xiǎng guo.
我 连 想 都 没 有 想 过。
I didn't even give it a thought.

Use of *bù guǎn........ dōu.......* (不管....都....) construction:

This construction is used to give the meaning "regardless of / no matter". Interrogatives are used after ***bù guǎn...... dōu......*** (不管.....都.....) structure. For example.

Bù guǎn nǐ qù bù qù, bié ren dōu yào qù.
不 管 你 去 不 去，别 人 都 要 去。
No matter you go or you don't go, others want to go.

Bù guǎn tā shì shéi, wǒ dōu bù tóng yī.
不 管 他 是 谁，我 都 不 同 意 。
No matter who he is, I don't agree.

Use of *zhèng zài* (正在) :

To show the progressive aspect of an action, the adverb ***zhèng zài*** (正在) is placed in front of the predicative verb. For example:

Tā men zhèng zài dǎ qiú ne.
他 们 正 在 打 求 呢 。
They are playing ball.

Tā zhèng zài shuì jiào ne.
他 正 在 睡 觉 呢 。
He is sleeping.

Use of *Chú le........ yǐ wài* (除 了 . . . . 以 外) structure:

Chú le.......yǐ wài (除 了 . . . . 以 外), means "except" or "besides". For example:

Chú le tā yǐ wài bíe ren dōu lái le.
除 了 他 以 外 别 人 都 来 了 。
Except him, others have all come.

Chú le Běi jīng yǐ wài, wǒ hái qù guò shàng hǎi.
除了北京 以外，我还去过 上 海。
Besides Beijing, I have also been to Shanghai.

Use of *Zhǐ yǒu...... cái......* (只有...才...) and *zhǐ yào....jiù...* (只要...就...) Structure:

Both ***zhǐ yǒu*** (只有)*and* ***zhǐ yào*** (只要) show a condition, but their difference is that ***zhǐ yǒu*** **(只有)** stresses this is the only condition and no other condition will do whereas ***zhǐ yào*** (只要) indicates it is enough to have this condition though there are still others. For example:

Zhǐ yǒu nǐ qīn zì gēn tā shuō, tā cái huì tóng yī qù.
只有你亲自跟他说，他才会同意去。
He won't agree to go unless you talk to him personally.

Zhǐ yào jì zhù zhè diǎn, jiù bù huì chū wèn tí.
知要记住 这 点，就 不会 出 问题。
As long as you remember this, there will be no problem.

REFERENCE I

Measure words
Liàng cí
量　词

One of the most difficult skills in Chinese is the use of measure words. Every noun has a specific measure word that is used to refer to it. The most commonly used measure word in Chinese is ***gè*** (个) which can refer to almost anything. However, use of proper measure word is more proper. Here is a list of some measure words and the nouns for which these are used:

Measure Word	*What It Modifies*	*Example*
Běn (本)	Book, Magazine, Dictionary etc.	*Yī* ***běn*** *shū* (A book)
Zhāng (张)	Map, Table, Photo, Bed, Painting etc.	*Zhè* ***Zhāng*** *huá* (This painting)
Bǎ (把)	Chair, Key, Knife.	*Liǎng* ***bǎ*** *dāo* (Two knives)
Zhī (支)	Writing tools.	*Sǎn* ***zhī*** *bǐ* (Three pens)
Tái (台)	Machines.	*Yī* ***tái*** *jì suàn jī* (A calculator)

***Lìang* (辆)**	Vehicles.	*Sì* ***liàng*** *qì chē* (Four cars)
***Fēng* (封)**	Letters.	*Nà* ***fēng*** *xìn* (That letter)
***Jiàn* (间)**	Rooms.	*Yī* ***jiàn*** *wò shì* (A bedroom)
***Jiàn* (件)**	Garments & dresses	*Wǔ* ***jiàn*** *dà yī* (Five overcoats)
***Kuài* (块)**	Money, soap, bread	*Shí* ***kuài*** *qián* (Ten Yuan)
***Tiáo* (条)**	Long, linear objects	*Sān* ***tiáo*** *yú* (Three fish)

REFERENCE II

Numbers & Quantities
Shù zì hé Shù Liàng
数 字 和 数 量

Cardinal Numbers
Jì shù
基 数

0	Zero	*lìng*	零
1	One	*yī*	一
2	Two	*èr*	二
3	Three	*sān*	三
4	Four	*sì*	四
5	Five	*wǔ*	五
6	Six	*lìu*	六
7	Seven	*qī*	七
8	Eight	*bā*	八
9	Nine	*jǐu*	九
10	Ten	*shí*	十

11	Eleven	*shí yī*	十一
12	Twelve	*shí èr*	十二
13	Thirteen	*shí sān*	十三
14	Fourteen	*shí sì*	十四
15	Fifteen	*shí wǔ*	十五
16	Sixteen	*shí lìu*	十六
17	Seventeen	*shí qī*	十七
18	Eighteen	*shí bā*	十八
19	Nineteen	*shí jǐu*	十九
20	Twenty	*èr shí*	二十
21	Twenty One	*èr shí yī*	二十一
30	Thirty	*sān shí*	三十
31	Thirty One	*sān shí yī*	三十一
40	Forty	*sì shí*	四十
41	Forty One	*sì shí yī*	四十一
50	Fifty	*wǔ shí*	五十
51	Fifty One	*wǔ shí yī*	五十一

60	Sixty	*lìu shí*	六 十
61	Sixty One	*lìu shí yī*	六 十 一
70	Seventy	*qī shí*	七 十
71	Seventy One	*qī shí yī*	七 十 一
80	Eighty	*bā shí*	八 十
81	Eighty One	*bā shí yī*	八 十 一
90	Ninety	*jǐu shí*	九 十
91	Ninety One	*jǐu shí yī*	九 十 一
100	Hundred	*yī bǎi*	一 百
101	Hundred One	*yī bǎi líng yī*	一 百 零 一
111	Hundred eleven	*yī bǎi yī shí yī*	一 百 一 十 一
150	Hundred Fifty	*yī bǎi wǔ shí*	一 百 五 十
199	Hundred Ninety Nine	*yī bǎi jǐu shí jǐu*	一 百 九 十 九
200	Two Hundred	*èr bǎi*	二 百
500	Five Hundred	*wǔ bǎi*	五 百
501	Five Hundred One	*wǔ bǎi líng yī*	五 百 零 一

1000	One Thousand	*yì qiān*	一 千
1001	One Thousand One	*yì qiān líng yī*	一 千 零 一
1500	One Thousand Five Hundred	*yì qiān wǔ bǎi*	一 千 五 百
1999	One Thousand Nine Hundred Ninety Nine	*yì qiān jǐu bǎi jǐu shí jǐu*	一 千 九 百 九 十 九
5000	Five Thousand	*wǔ qiān*	五 千
9999	Nine Thousand Nine Hundred Ninety Nine	*jǐu qiān jǐu bǎi jǐu shí jǐu*	九 千 九 百 九 十 九
10,000	Ten Thousand	*yí wàn*	一 万
100,000	Hundred Thousand	*shí wàn*	十 万
1,000,000	One Million	*bǎi wàn*	百 万
10,000,000	Ten Million	*qiān wàn*	千 万
100,000,000	Hundred Million	*yí yì*	一 亿
1,000,000,000	One Billion	*shí yì*	十 亿
10,000,000,000	Ten Billion	*yì bǎi yì*	一 百 亿

Ordinal Numbers
Xù shù
序 数

First	*Dì yī*	第 一
Second	*Dì èr*	第 二
Third	*Dì sān*	第 三
First One	*Dì yī gè*	第 一 个
Second One	*Dì èr gè*	第 二 个
Third One	*Dì sān gè*	第 三 个
First Time	*Dì yī cì*	第 一 次
Second Time	*Dì èr cì*	第 二 次
Third Time	*Dì sān cì*	第 三 次

Fractions
Fēn shù
分 数

1/2	*èr fēn zhī yī*	二 分 之 一
1/4	*Sì fēn zhī yī*	四 分 之 一
2/3	*Sān fēn zhī èr*	三 分 之 二
3/4	*Sì fēn zhī sān*	四 分 之 三

Percentages
Bǎi fēn shù
百 分 数

11%	*Bǎi fēn zhī shí yī*	百分之十一
18.4%	*Bǎi fēn zhī shí bā diǎn sì*	百分之十八点四
25%	*Bǎi fēn zhī èr shí wǔ*	百分之二十五
50%	*Bǎi fēn zhī wǔ shí*	百分之五十
75%	*Bǎi fēn zhī qī shí wǔ*	百分之七十五
100%	*Bǎi fēn zhī yī bǎi*	百分之一百

REFERENCE III

Days, Months & Seasons
Xīng qī, Yuè fèn hé Jì jié
星期，月份和季节

Days of the week
Xīng qī
星期

Sunday	*xīng qī tīan*	星期天
Monday	*xīng qī yī*	星期一
Tuesday	*xīng qī èr*	星期二
Wednesday	*xīng qī sān*	星期三
Thursday	*xīng qī sì*	星期四
Friday	*xīng qī wǔ*	星期五
Saturday	*xīng qī lìu*	星期六

Months
Yùe fèn
月份

January	*yī yuè*	一月
February	*èr yuè*	二月

March	*sān yuè*	三 月
April	*sì yuè*	四 月
May	*wǔ yuè*	五 月
June	*lìu yue*	六 月
July	*qī yuè*	七 月
August	*bā yuè*	八 月
September	*jǐu yuè*	九 月
October	*shí yuè*	十 月
November	*shí yī yuè*	十 一 月
December	*shí èr yuè*	十 二 月

Seasons of the year
Jì jié
季 节

Spring	*chūn jì*	春 季
Summer	*xià jì*	夏 季
Rainy	*yǔ jì*	雨 季
Autumn	*qīu jì*	秋 季
Winter	*dōng jì*	冬 季

REFERENCE IV

Measures & Weights
Dù Liàng
度 量

Weight
Zhòng liàng
重 量

Ligram	*háo kè*	毫克
Centigram	*lí kè*	厘克
Decigram	*fēn kè*	分克
Gram	*kè*	克
Decagram	*shí k*	十克
Hectogram	*bǎi kè*	百克
Kilogram	*qīan kè*	千克
Quintal	*gōng dàn*	公担
Metric Ton	*gōng tùn*	公吨
Pound	*bàng*	磅
Ounce	*àng sı*	盎司

Capacity
Róng Liàng
容 量

Microlitre	*wēi shēng*	微 升
Millilitre	*háo shēng*	毫 升
Centilitre	*lı shēng*	厘 升
Decilitre	*fēn shēng*	分 升
Litre	*shēng*	升
Decalitre	*shí shēng*	十 升
Hectolitre	*bǎi shēng*	百 升
Kilolitre	*qiān shēng*	千 升
Gallon	*jiā lún*	加 仑

Length
Cháng dù
长 度

Millimicron	*háo wēi mǐ*	毫 微 米
Micron	*wēi mǐ*	微 米
Centimillimetre	*hū mǐ*	忽 米
Decimillimetre	*sī mǐ*	丝 米
Millimetre	*háo mǐ*	毫 米

Centimetre	*lí mǐ*	厘 米
Square centimetre	*píng fāng lí mǐ*	平 方 厘 米
Decimetre	*fēn mǐ*	分 米
Metre	*mǐ*	米
Decametre	*shí mǐ*	十 米
Hectometre	*bái mǐ*	百 米
Kilometre	*gōng li*	公 里
Mile	*yīng lǐ*	英 里
Square mile	*píng fāng yīng lǐ*	平 方 英 里
Nautical mile	*hái lǐ*	海 里
Yard	*mǎ*	码
Square yard	*píng fāng mǎ*	平 方 码
Foot	*yīng chǐ*	英 尺
Square foot	*pìng fāng yīng chǐ*	平 方 英 尺
Inch	*yīng cùn*	英 寸
Square inch	*píng fāng yīng cùn*	平 方 英 寸
Acre	*yīng mu*	英 亩
Hectare	*gōng qing*	公 顷

CHAPTER I

General Expressions
Cháng yòng yǔ
常　用　语

Hello!
Nǐ hǎo!
你 好！
You good

Please.
Qǐng.
请。

Excuse me.
Láo jià.
劳　驾。

Yes.
Shì.
是。

No.
Bú shì.
不 是。

Thank you!
Xìe xìe nǐ!
谢 谢 你！
Thank you

It's all right.
Bíe kè qì.
别 客 气。
Not polite

Sorry!
Duì bù qǐ!
对 不 起！

Never mind.
Meí guān xì.
没 关 系。
No matter

Pardon me.
Qǐng yuàn liàng.
请 原 谅。
Please pardon

Please have a seat.
Qǐng zuò.
请 坐。
Please to sit.

Please come in.
Qǐng jìn.
请　进。
Please　to enter

Please wait for a while.
Qǐng shāo děng.
请　稍　等。
Please　little　to wait

How are you?
Nǐ hǎo ma?
你　好　吗？
You　good

Fine, Thank you!
Hái hǎo, xìe xìe!
还　好，谢　谢！
Still good　Thanks

How is your health?
Shēn tǐ zěn me yàng?
身　体　怎　么　样？
Health　how

Are you busy?
Máng ma?
忙 吗？
Busy

What is your surname?
Nín guì xìng?
您 贵 姓？
You valuable surname

I am from India.
Wǒ shì Yìn dù rén.
我 是 印 度 人。
I am Indian

Welcome.
Huān yíng.
欢 迎。
Welcome

Congratulations!
Gōng xǐ gōng xǐ!
恭 喜 恭 喜！
Congratulations

Good-bye!
Zài jiàn!
再 见！
Again see

See you tomorrow!
Míng tiān jiàn!
明 天 见！
Tomorrow to see

Which country are you from?
Nǐ shì nǎ guó rén?
你 是 哪 国 人？
You are which country person

I am glad to meet you.
Hěn gāo xìng jiàn dào nín.
很 高 兴 见 到 您。
Very glad to see you.

What is your name?
Nǐ jiào shén me míng zì?
你 叫 什 么 名 字？
You called what name

How old are you? (for asking children)
Nǐ jǐ suì le?
你 几 岁 了？
You what age

How old are you? (for asking adults)
Nǐ duō dà le?
你 多 大 了？
You how big

How old are you? (for asking elders)
Nín duō dà nián jì le?
您 多 大 年 纪 了？
You how big age

I am 30 years old.
Wǒ sān shí le.
我 三 十 了。
I thirty

How many members are there in your family?
Nǐ jiā yǒu jǐ kǒu rén?
你 家 有 几 口 人？
You family have how many persons

There are three members in our family.
Wǒ jiā yǒu sān kǒu rén.
我 家 有 三 口 人。
I family have three persons.

Please have a cup of tea/ coffee/ a glass of water/ a soft drink.
Qǐng he bei chá / kā fēi / kāi shuǐ / léng yǐn.
请 喝 杯 茶 咖啡 开 水 冷 饮。
Please to drink cup tea coffee boiled water soft drink

I don't take hot water, I want mineral water.
Wǒ bù hē kāi shuǐ, wǒ hē kuàng quán shuǐ.
我 不 喝 开 水，我 喝 矿 泉 水。
I no to drink boiled water I to drink mineral water

Do you smoke?
Nǐ chōu yān ma?
你 抽 烟 吗？
You to smoke cigarette

Please have a cigarette.
Qǐng chōu yān.
请 抽 烟
Please to smoke cigarette

Do you drink?
Nǐ hē jǐu ma?
你 喝 酒 吗？
You to drink wine.

Please have some beer/ wine/ liquor/ Champaign.
Qǐng hē pí jǐu / pú táo jǐu / bái jǐu / xiāng bīn.
请 喝 啤酒 葡萄酒 白酒 香 槟。
Please to drink beer grape wine liquor champaign

Please allow me to introduce.
Qǐng ràng wǒ jìe shào yí xià.
请 让 我 介绍 一下。
Please let me to introduce a while

This is Mrs..... / Mr. .... / Ms........
Zhè wèi shì ..... fū rén / ...... xiān sheng / ....xiáo jǐe.
这 位 是 ...夫 人 / ... 先 生 / ...小姐。
This is .... Mrs. ....Mr. ,,,,,,,,Ms.

Have you come alone / with wife (husband)?
Nǐ shì yí gè rén / gēn fū rén (zhàng fū) yì qǐ lái de?
你 是 一个 人 / 跟 夫人 （丈夫） 一起 来的？
You are one person with wife (husband) together to come

How about your journey?
Nǐ men lái de hái shùn lì ma?
你们 来的 还 顺 利 吗？
You to come still smooth

We had a comfortable / tiring journey.
Yí lù shàng hěn shùn lì / bú shì tài shùn lì.
一路 上 很 顺 利 / 不 是 太 顺 利。
Journey on very smooth not is very smooth

What is our programme?
Wǒ men jì huà gàn shén me?
我们 计划 干 什 么？
We a plan to do what

What is our travel schedule?
Wǒ men de lǚ xíng shì zěn me ān pái de?
我们 的 旅行 是 怎么 安排 的？
Ours travel is how to arrange

I am a businessman / doctor / journalist / engineer.
Wǒ shì shāng rén / yī shēng / jì zhě / gōng chéng shī.
我 是 商 人 / 医生 / 记者 / 工 程 师。
I am trader doctor reporter engineer

We are members of a science / trade delegation.
Wǒ men shì kē xué / mào yì dài biǎo tuán chéng yuán.
我们 是 科学/ 贸 易 代 表 团 成 员。
We are science trade delegation member

I can't speak Chinese.
Wǒ bù hùi jiǎng Zhōng wén.
我 不 会 讲 中 文。
I not can speak Chinese.

Can you speak English?
Nǐ néng shuō yīng yǔ ma?
你 能 说 英 语 吗?
You can speak English

This is my first trip to China.
Zhè shì wǒ dì yī cì dào Zhōng guó.
这 是 我 第一次 到 中 国。
This is I the first to reach China

Would you please repeat that?
Láo jià nǐ zài shuō yí biàn?
劳 驾 你 在 说 一 遍?
Pardon you again to speak once.

What does this word mean?
Zhè gè zì shì shén me yì sī?
这 个 字 是 什 么 意思?
This word is what meaning

How do we pronounce this word?
Zhè gè zì zěn men niàn?
这个字怎么念？
This word how to read

Are you married?
Nǐ jíe hūn le ma?
你结婚了吗？
You married

I am married. I have two children.
Jié le. Wǒ yǒu liǎng gè hái zi.
结了。我有两个孩子。
Married I have two children

Where do you work?
Nǐ zài nǎ li zuò shì?
你在哪里做事？
You at where to work

My office is in New Delhi.
Wǒ de bàn gōng shì zài Xīn dé lǐ.
我的班公室在新德里。
My office at New Delhi

We don't have any branch / representative office in China.
Wǒ men zài Zhōng guó hái méi yǒu kāi shè
我 们 在 中 国 还 没 有 开 设
We at China still not have to start

fēn gōng sī / dài biǎo chù.
分 公 司/ 代 表 处。
branch representative office

I am a manager / technician.
Wǒ shì jīng lǐ / jì shù rén yuán.
我 是 经 理 / 技 术 人 员。
I am manager technical personnel

Let's toast for good health / happiness / success.
Ràng wǒ men wèi jiàn kāng /xìng fú /chéng gōng gān bēi!
让 我 们 为 健 康 / 幸 福 / 成 功 干 杯!
Let we for goodhealth happiness success cheers

Happy Journey.
Yí lù píng ān.
一 路 平 安。
Safe journey

CHAPTER II

At The Airport
Zài Jī chǎng
在 机 场

Entry
Rù jìng
入 境

A: May I have a look at your passport and visa?
Qǐng kàn yí xià nín de hù zhào hé qiān zhèng.
请 看一下 您 的 护照 和 签 证。
Please have a look yours passport and visa

B: Here is my passport and visa.
Zhè shì wǒ de hù zhào hé qiān zhèng.
这 是 我 的 护照 和 签 证。
This is my passport and visa

A: May I have a look at your vaccination certificate?
Qǐng chū shì nín de fáng yì zhèng.
请 出示 您 的 防疫症。
Please to show your vaccination certificate

B: Here is my vaccination certificate.

Zhè shì wǒ de fáng yì zhèng.

这 是 我 的 防 疫 症。

This is my vaccination certificate

A: How long will you stay here?

Nín zài zhè er dòu líu jǐ tiān?

您 在 这儿 逗 留 几天。

You at here to stay how many days

B: I'll stay here for one day / a week / two weeks / a month.

Wǒ zài zhè er dāi yì tiān/ yì zhōu/ liǎng zhōu/ yí gè yuè.

我 在 这儿 待 一天/ 一 周/ 两 周/ 一个月。

I at here to stay a day a week a fornight a month

A: What is the purpose of your visit here?

Nín lái zùo shén me?

您 来 做 什 么？

You come to do what

B: I am here for holiday / business.

Wǒ lái zhè er lǔ yóu / zùo shēng yì.

我 来 这儿 旅 游/ 做 生 意。

I come here to travel to do business

Customs
Hǎi guān
海　关

A:　Please fill in the form.

Qǐng tián yì xià zhè zhāng biǎo.

请　填　一下　这　张　表。

Please　to fill　a while　this　form

B:　I have nothing to declare.

Wǒ méi yǒu shén me yào shēn bào de.

我　没　有　什　么　要　申　报　的。

I　don't have　anything　want　to declare

I have a watch / a tape recorder/ a TV /a camera.

Wǒ yǒu shǒu biǎo/ lù yīn jī/ diàn shì jī/ zhào xiàng jī.

我　有　手　表/ 录音机/电　视　机/ 照　相　机。

I　have wristwatch　taperecorder　television　camera

It is for my own use.

Zhè shì wǒ zì jǐ yòng de.

这　是　我　自己　用　的。

It　is　my　own　to use

It is not new.

Zhè bú shì xīn de.

这　不是　新　的。

It　not　is　new one

This is a gift for others.

Zhè shì sòng rén de lǐ wù.

这 是 送 人 的 礼物。

This is to give person a gift

Should I have to pay a duty on this?

Wǒ yìng gāi jiāo shuì ma?

我 应 该 交 税 吗？

I should to pay duty

Exit

Chū jìng

出 境

A: Have you paid the airport tax?

Jī chǎng jiàn shè fèi nín fù le méi yǒu?

机 场 建 设 费 您 付 了 没 有？

Airport tax you to pay not

B: No, I haven't yet. How much is the tax?

Hái méi yǒu. Yào fù duō shǎo?

还 没 有。要 付 多 少？

Yet not want to pay how much

A: It's ninety yuan. Please pay it near the entrance gate.

Jǐu shí kuài Rén mín bì. Qǐng dào rù kǒu chù jiāo qián.

九 十 块 人 民 币。请 到 入 口 处 交 钱。

Ninety yuan RMB please to entrance pay money

Please show me your declaration form.
Qǐng kàn yí xià nín de shēn bào dān.
请 看一下 您 的 申 报 单。
Please to look yours declaration form

B: Here is my declaration form.
Zhè shì wǒ de shēn bào dān.
这 是 我 的 申 报 单。
This is my declaration form

A: Please show me the valuable things you brought in.
Qǐng gěi wǒ kàn yí xià nín rù jìng shí dài lái
请 给 我 看一下 您 入境 时 带 来
May to give I have a look you entry time brought in

de guì zhòng wù pǐn.
的 贵 重 物品。
valuable things

B: Here are the things.
Zhè jìu shì.
这 就 是。
This just is

A: Do you still have this article / thing?
Zhè jiàn dōng xi hái zài ma?
这 件 东 西 还 在 吗?
This thing still there

B: I don't have it.

Bú zài le.

不 在 了。

Not here

A: Have this article been given away / have you lost it?

Zhè gè dōng xi nín sōng rén le / dīu le?

这 个 东 西 您 送 人 了/ 丢 了?

This thing you to gift person lost

B: I have given it away / lost it.

Wǒ sōng rén le / dīu le.

我 送 人 了/ 丢 了。

I to gift person lost

A: Do you have a certificate for the loss?

Yǒu méi yǒu yí shī zhèng míng?

有 没 有 遗 失 证 明?

Have not have to lose certificate

B: This is the certificate for the loss.

Zhè jìu shì yí shī zhèng míng.

这 就 是 遗 失 证 明。

This just is to lose certificate

A: You must pay duty for this article.
Nín děi jiāo shuì.
您 得 交 税。
You must to pay tax

B: How much is the duty?
Yào jiāo duō shǎo?
要 交 多 少？
Want to pay how much

A: The duty is .... yuan.
Shùi é shì .... Yuān.
税 额 是.... 元。
Tax volume is ... yuan

Addl. - Vocabulary

Flight Ticket	*jī piào*	机 票
Flight Number	*háng bān*	航 班
Boarding Pass	*dēng jī pái*	登 机 牌
Security Check	*ān quán jiǎn chá*	安 全 检 查
Luggage	*xíng lǐ*	行 李

Baggage Tag	*xíng lǐ biāo qiān*	行李标签
Trolley	*tuī chē*	推车
Custom Officer	*hǎi guān guān yuán*	海关官员
Red Channel	*hóng sè tōng dào*	红色通道
Green Channel	*lǜ sè tōng dào*	绿色通道
Money Exchange Counter	*wài huì duì huàn chù*	外汇兑换处
Public Telephone	*gōng yòng diàn huà*	公用电话
Duty Free Shop	*miǎn shuì shāng diàn*	免税商店
Tourist Visa	*lǚ yóu qiān zhèng*	旅游签证
Business Visa	*shāng wù qiān zhèng*	商务签证

China International Travel Service (CITS)
Zhōng guó guó jì lǚ xíng shè (guó lǚ)
中国 国际 旅行社 （国旅）

CHAPTER III

Hiring A Taxi
Chū zū qì chē
出 租 汽 车

Where can I get a taxi?
Chū zū qì chē zài nǎ er ?
出租汽车 在 哪儿?
Taxi at where

Please get me a taxi.
Qǐng bāng wǒ zhǎo yí xià chū zū qì chē.
请 帮 我 找一下 出租汽车。
Please help me to find taxi

Could you help me to carry my luggage?
Nín néng bāng wǒ tí xíng lǐ ma?
您 能 帮 我 提 行 李 吗?
You can to help me to carry luggage

Take me to Beijing University please.
Qǐng dào Běi jīng dà xué.
请 到 北京大学。
Please to reach Beijing University

How far is it to Beijing University?

Dào Běi jīng dà xué yào duō yuǎn?

到 北京 大学 要 多 远？

To Beijing University require how far

Where are we now?

Wǒ men xiàn zài zài nǎ er ?

我们 现在 在 哪儿？

We at present at where

Have we reached?

Wǒ men dào le ma?

我们 到 了 吗？

We reached

How much is it?

Duō shao qián?

多 少 钱？

How much money

Keep the change.

Bié zhǎo le.

别 找 了。

No return

Give me the change please.

Qǐng zhǎo qián.

请 找 钱。

Please return money

I am in hurry, please drive fast.
Wǒ yǒu jí shì, qǐng kāi kuài diǎn.
我 有 急事，请 开 快 点。
I have urgent work please drive fast a bit.

Is your meter working?
Zhè gè jì chéng biǎo zǒu de duì ma?
这 个 计程 表 走 的 对 吗？
This meter to run right

Please wait for a minute.
Qǐng nǐ děng yí xià.
请 你 等 一 下。
Please you to wait a while

Please pick me up tomorrow morning at nine o'clock.
Qǐng míng tiān zǎo shang jiǔ diǎn zhōng lái zhè er jīe wǒ.
请 明 天 早 上 九 点 钟 来 这儿 接 我。
Please tomorrow morning 9.00A.M. to come here fetch me

CHAPTER IV

At the Hotel
Zài lǚ guǎn
在 旅馆

Check-in
Dēng jì
登 记

A: Good morning!
Zǎo shang hǎo!
早 上 好！
Morning good

B: Good morning!
Zǎo shang hǎo!
早 上 好！
Morning good

A: Can I get a room here?
Zhè lǐ yǒu fáng jiān ma?
这 里 有 房 间 吗？
Here have room

B: Sir, do you have any reservation with us?
Qǐng wèn nín yù dìng le méi yǒu?
请 问 您 预 订 了 没 有？
Please ask you advance book not have

A: No, I have not made any reservation.
Méi yǒu, Wǒ méi yǒu yù dìng.
没 有，我 没 有 预 订。
Not have I not have advance book

B: For how many days do you want to stay here?
Nín zhǔn bèi zài zhè lǐ dāi jǐ tiān?
您 准 备 在 这 里 待 几 天？
You to prepare at here to stay how many days

A: For six days.
Lìu tiān.
六 天。
Six days

B: Sir, you want double or single room?
Nín xiǎng yào dān rén hái shì shuāng rén fáng jiān?
您 想 要 单 人 还 是 双 人 房 间？
You to think want one person or two persons room

A: I want a single room.
Wǒ xiǎng yào Dān rén jiān.
我 想 要 单 人 间。
I to think want one person room

B: AC room or non-AC room?
Yào dài kōng tiáo de hái shì bú dài kōng tiáo de?
要带 空 调 的 还是 不带 空 调 的?
Want to have air-condition or not to have air-condition

A: I want AC room.
Yào dài kōng tiáo de.
要 带 空 调 的。
Want have air-condition

B: Yes, you can get a room here.
Kě yǐ , nín kě yǐ zài zhè er zhù.
可以，您 可以 在 这儿 住。
May you can at here stay

A: How much is the room rate?
Fáng jià duō shao?
房 价 多 少?
Room rate how much

B: It is 500 yuan per day plus taxes.
Wǔ bǎi yuán yì tiān , hái jiā shuì.
五 百 元 一天 ，还 加 税。
500 yuan one day still to add tax

A: Is it twin bedded or single bed room?
Fáng jiān lǐ yǒu liǎng chuáng hái shì yì chuáng?
房 间 里 有 两 床 还是 一 床?
Room inside have two beds or single bed

B: It is twin bedded.

Liǎng zhāng chuáng.

两 张 床。

Two beds

A: Can I get a large bed?

Wǒ néng yào yì zhāng dà chuáng ma?

我 能 要 一张 大床 吗？

I can ask for one large bed

B: Sorry sir! It is not available at the moment.

Duì bù qǐ! Xiàn zài zàn shí méi yǒu.

对不起！先在 暂时 没有。

Sorry at present for the time being not have

A: Can I see the room?

Wǒ néng xiān kàn yí xià fáng jiān ma?

我 能 先 看一下 房间 吗？

I can first to have a look room

I don't like the room. Do you have any other better room?

Wǒ bù xǐ huān zhè jiān fáng. Nǐ hái yǒu

我 不 喜欢 这 间 房。你 还有

I not like this room you still have

gèng hǎo de fáng jiān ma?

更 好 的 房间 吗？

better room

I want a pool side room.
Wǒ yào yì jiān kào yǒng chí de fáng jiān.
我 要 一 间 靠 泳 池 的 房 间。
I want one near swimming pool's room

B: Sorry! All the rooms on that side are occupied.
Duì bù qǐ! nà biān de fáng jiān dōu mǎn le.
对不起！那 边 的 房 间 都 满 了。
Sorry that side room all occupied

A: O.K., I will take this room.
Xíng, wǒ jìu zhù zhè er.
行， 我 就 住 这 儿。
O.K. I just to stay here

B: Can I have your name please?
Qǐng wèn nín de míng zì?
请 问 您 的 名 字？
Please ask your name

Where are you coming from?
Nín cóng nǎ er lái?
您 从 哪 儿 来？
You from where to come

What is your next destination?
Nín hái xiǎng dào nǎ er qù?
您 还 想 到 哪 儿 去？
You still to think to where to go

Would you please sign here sir?
Qǐng nín zài zhè lǐ qiān zì.
请 您 在 这里 签 字。
Please you at here to sign

Thank you. Your room number is 101.
Xìe xìe nín. Nín de fáng jiān hào shì yāo líng yāo.
谢谢 您。您 的 房 间 号 是 一零一。
Thank you yours room number is 101

A: Is it on the 1st floor?
Shì zài yī lóu ma?
是 在 一楼 吗？
Is at 1st floor

B: No, sir, it's on the second floor.
Bù, shì zài èr lóu.
不，是 在 二楼。
No is at 2nd floor

A: Does this room have TV and refrigerator?
Zhè jiān fáng yǒu diàn shì hé bīng xiāng ma?
这 间 房 有 电 视 和 冰 箱 吗？
This room have TV and refrigerator

Is hot water available in the bathroom?
Kě yǐ xǐ rè shuǐ ma?
可以 洗 热水 吗？
Can to wash hot water

B: Yes sir. All these facilities are there.
Kě yǐ. Zhè lǐ yīng yǒu jìn yǒu.
可以。这里 应 有 尽 有。
Can here should have all have

A: Do you have Internet facility in the hotel?
Fàn diàn lǐ kě yǐ shàng Guó jì hù lián wǎng ma?
饭 店 里 可以 上 国 际 互 联 网 吗？
Hotel inside can on internet

B: Yes sir, it is available on request.
Kě yǐ. Nín děi shì xiān shēn qǐng.
可以。您 得 事 先 申 请。
Can you should matter first to apply for

A: Can I make international call from here?
Néng dǎ guó jì cháng tú diàn huà ma?
能 打 国 际 长 途 电 话 吗？
Can make international long distance telephone

B: Yes. You can make it through operator.
Nín kě yǐ tōng guò jīe xiàn yuán dǎ.
您 可以 通 过 接 线 员 打。
You can through operator to make a call

A: What are the per minute charges?
Yī fēn zhōng duō shao qián?
一 分 钟 多 少 钱？
One minute how much money

B: The charges are US$6 per minute.
Měi fēn zhōng lìu měi yuán.
每 分 钟 六 美 元。
Each minute six US$

A: What are the timings for the swimming pool/ discotheque / bar/ restaurant / health club?
Yóu yǒng chí /dí tīng / jǐu bā / cān tīng /jiàn shēn fáng
游 泳 池/ 迪厅/ 酒 吧/ 餐 厅/ 健 身 房
Swimming pool disco hall bar restaurant health club

shén me shí hòu kāi fàng?
什 么 时 后 开 放？
what time open

Where is the elevator?
Diàn tī zài nǎ er?
电 梯 在 哪 儿？
Lift at where

B: You go straight then turn left, there you are.
Wǎng qián zǒu, zài wǎng yòu yì guǎi jìu dào le.
往 前 走，在 往 右 一拐 就 到 了。
Towards front to walk then towards right to turn just reached

A: Could you help sending my luggage to the room?
Nǐ néng bāng wǒ bǎ xíng lǐ sòng dào fáng jiān ma?

你 能 帮 我 把 行李 送 到 房 间 吗?

You can to help me let luggage send to room

B: Don't worry sir, it will reach your room.
Bíe dān xīn xiān sheng, jì kè sòng dào nín

别 胆 心 先 生, 即刻 送 到 您

Not worry Mr./ sir immediately send to yours

de fáng jiān.

的 房 间。

room

A: Thank you!
Xìe xìe!

谢 谢!

Thanks

B: You are welcome, sir.
Bíe kè qì, xiān sheng.

别 客气, 先 生。

Not polite Mr. / sir

Using Hotel Service
Kè fáng fú wù
客房 服务

A: Is it House Keeping? Please pick up my laundry.
Shì kè fáng bù ma ? Qǐng nǐ men ná qù wǒ
是 客房 部 吗? 请 你们 拿去 我
Is room service please you pick to go I

yào xǐ de yī fu.
要 洗 的 衣服。
want to wash clothes

B: Please leave your clothes in the laundry bag, sir.
Qǐng bǎ yī fu fàng jìn xǐ yī dài lǐ.
请 把 衣服 房 进 洗衣袋 里。
Please let clothes put into laundry bag inside

A: When will it be ready?
Shén me shí hòu néng sòng húi lai?
什么 时候 能 送回来?
What time can to return

B: It will be ready by tomorrow afternoon sir.
Míng tiān xià wǔ, xiān sheng.
明天 下午, 先生。
Tomorrow afternoon sir

A: I want it as soon as possible.
Wǒ xiǎng jìn kuài shōu dào.
我 想 尽快 收 到。
I to think as soon as possible to receive

Is it Room Service? I will take dinner in my room. Please take the order.
Shì kè fáng bù ma? Wǒ xiǎng zài fáng jiān
是 客 房 部 吗？我 想 在 房 间
Is room service I want at room

yòng wǎn cān.
用 晚 餐。
to take dinner

B: At what time will you take dinner sir?
Nín xiǎng zài shén me shí hòu yòng
您 想 在 什 么 时 候 用
You think at what time to take

wǎn cān, xiān sheng?
晚 餐， 先 生？
dinner sir

A: At eight o'clock.
Wǎn shang bā diǎn.
晚 上， 八 点。
Evening eight o'clock

A: Is it Reception? Please wake me up at 6:30 in the morning.
Shì zǒng tái ma? Qǐng míng tiān zǎo shang
是 总 台 吗？请 明 天 早 上
Is reception please tomorrow morning

lìu diǎn bàn jiào xǐng wǒ.
六 点 半 叫 醒 我。
6:30 call wake me

Could you help me to open my room? I have left the key inside the room.
Nǐ néng bāng wǒ dǎ kāi fáng jiān ma?
你 能 帮 我 打 开 房 间 吗？
You can help me open room

Wǒ bǎ yào shi suǒ zài fáng lǐ le.
我 把 钥 匙 锁 再 房 里 了。
I let door key to lock at room inside

Is there any message / mail for me?
Yǒu gěi wǒ de líu yán / xìn ma?
有 给 我 的 留 言 / 信 吗？
Have give my message letter

Please keep my bill ready.
Qǐng zhǔn bèi jié zhàng.
请 准 备 结 帐。
Please to prepare to clear bill

Checking Out
Tuì fáng
退 房

A: Can I have my bill please? I want to check out.
Néng bǎ zhàng dān gěi wǒ ma? Wǒ yào tuì fáng.
能 把 帐 单 给 我 吗？我 要 退 房。
Could let bill to give me I want check out

B: What is your room number, sir?
Nín de fáng jiān hào shì duō shao, xiān sheng?
您 的 房 间 号 是 多 少，先 生？
Your room number is how much sir

A: My room number is 101.
Wǒ de fáng jiān hào shì yāo líng yāo.
我 的 房 间 号 是 一 零 一。
My room number is 101

B: This is your bill sir.
Zhè shì nín de zhàng dān.
这 是 您 的 帐 单。
This is your bill

A: Can I pay through traveller's cheque / Credit card?
Wǒ néng yòng lǚ xíng zhī piào/ xìn yòng kǎ zhī fù ma?
我 能 用 旅 行 支 票/ 信 用 卡 支 付 吗？
I can to use travel cheque credit card make payment

B: You can pay by credit card.

Nín kě yǐ yòng xìn yòng kǎ zhī fù.

您 可以 用 信 用 卡 支付。

You may use credit card make payment

Please deposit your room key.

Qǐng bǎ fáng jiān yào shi líu xià.

请 把 房 间 钥 匙 留 下。

Please let room key to leave

A: Would you send someone to bring my luggage down?

Nǐ néng jiào rén bān yùn wǒ de xíng li ma?

你 能 叫 人 搬 运 我 的 行 李 吗?

You can call person to carry my luggage

B: Right sir. Did you have a nice stay in the hotel?

Méi wèn tí. Nín zài zhè er zhù de hái hǎo ma?

没 问 题。您 在 这儿 住 的 还 好 吗?

No problem you at here to stay still good

A: Yes. It was very comfortable.

Hén hǎo. Zhè lǐ fei cháng shū shi.

很 好。这 里 非 常 舒 适。

Very good here extremely comfortable

B: Thank you sir. Have a nice day!

Xìe xìe nín xiān sheng. Zhù nín shùn lì!

谢 谢 您，先 生。祝 您 顺 利!

Thank you sir to wish you smooth

Addl. Vocabulary

Information Desk	*wěn xùn chù*	问讯处
Bell Boy	*xíng lǐ yuán*	行李员
Travel Desk	*lǚ xíng dài bàn chù*	旅行代办处
Lobby Manager	*dà táng jīng lǐ*	大堂经理
Standard Room	*biāo zhǔn jiān*	标准间
Deluxe Room	*háo huá jiān*	豪华间
Suite	*tào jiān*	套间
Guest House	*zhāo dài suǒ*	招待所
Front Office	*qián tái*	前台
Food & Beverages	*yǐn shí*	饮食
Banquet Hall	*yàn huì tīng*	宴会厅
Shopping Plaza	*gòu wù zhōng xīn*	购物中心
Gymnasium	*jiàn shēn fáng*	健身房
Buffet	*zì zhù cān*	自助餐
a la carte	*àn cài dān diǎn cài*	按菜单点菜
Menu Card	*cài dān*	菜单

CHAPTER V

Making A Telephone Call
Dǎ diàn huà
打 电 话

A: Is there any public telephone booth nearby?
Fù jìn yǒu gōng yòng diàn huà ma?
附近 有 公用 电话 吗?
Nearby have public telephone

Excuse me, can I make a local call from here?
Qǐng wèn, wǒ néng zài zhè er dǎ shì nèi diàn huà ma?
请问,我能 在 这儿 打 市内 电 话 吗?
Please tell I can at here to make local telephone

B: Sure.
Dāng rán kě yǐ.
当 然 可 以。
Of course

A: Could you tell me the number of People's University?
Nǐ néng gào sù wǒ Rén mín dà xué de
你 能 告 诉 我 人 民 大 学 的
You can tell me People's University's

diàn huà hào mǎ ma?
电 话 号 码 吗？
telephone number

B: The switchboard number is.......
Zǒng jī hào mǎ shì ....
总 机 号码 是........。
Switchboard number is....

A: Hello, please put me to foreign students hostel building.
Wèi, qǐng zhuǎn líu xué shēng lóu.
喂，请 转 留学生 楼。
Hello please to transfer foreign students building

Hello, could I speak to Indian student Ms. Sharma of room no.45?
Wèi, qǐng jiào yí xià sì shí wǔ hào fáng de
喂，请 叫 一下 四十五 号 房 的
Hello please to call a while forty five number room's

Yìn dù xué shēng, Xià ér mǎ xiǎo jǐe ma?
印度 学生，夏尔马 小 姐 吗？
Indian student Sharma Ms.

B: Hold the line.(after a while) She is not there. Please call after some time.
Bíe guà. (guò le yì huì r) Tā bú zài. Qǐng yǐ hòu zài dǎ lái.
别 挂。（过了一会儿）她不 在。请 以后 在 打来。
Hold on (after a while) she not there please after again make call

A: Can I make an International call from here?
Wǒ néng zài zhèer dǎ guójì chángtú diànhuà ma?
我 能 在 这儿 打 国际 长途 电话 吗？
I can at here make int'l long distance phone call

B: Yes, you can. Where do you want to call?
Kě yǐ. Nǐ yào dá nǎ er?
可以。你 要 打 哪儿？
Can you want make where

A: To New Delhi, India.
Yìn dù, Xīn dé lǐ.
印 度，新 德 里。
India New Delhi

Can I make a collect call?
Wǒ néng dǎ duì fāng fù kuǎn diàn huà ma?
我 能 打 对 方 付 款 电 话 吗？
I can to make other side make payment phone call

B: Sorry, this facility is not available.
Duì bù qǐ, zhè er méi yǒu zhè gè yè wù.
对 不 起，这 儿 没 有 这 个 业 务。
Sorry here not have this facility

The line is busy. Please dial after some time.
Diàn huà zhàn xiàn. Qǐng shāo hui zài dǎ.
电 话 占 线。请 稍 会 在 打。
Phone line busy please a while again call

The area code has changed. Please dial new area code.
Qū hào yǐ gēng gǎi. Qǐng bō xīn qū hào.
区号 已 更 改。请 拨 新 区 号。
Area code already change please dial new area code

A: Hello, is this Mr. Rao?
Wèi, qǐng wèn nǐ shì Lā ào xiān sheng ma?
喂，请 问 你 是 拉奥 先 生 吗？
Hello please tell you are Rao Mr.

I can't hear you! Please speak louder!
Wǒ tīng bú jiàn! Qǐng dà diǎn shēng!
我 听 不 见！请 大 点 声！
I can't hear please loud a bit voice

B: Have you finished?
Nǐ dǎ wàn le ma?
你 打 完 了 吗？
You call finished

A: Yes. How much is the bill?
Dǎ wán le. Duō shao qián?
打 完 了。多 少 钱？
Call finished how much money

B: You have talked for three minutes. The total bill is 75RMB.
Nǐ dǎ le sān fēn zhōng. Zǒng gòng qī shí wǔ yuán Rén mín bì.
你打了三分钟。总 共 七十五元 人民币。
You called three minutes all together seventy five yuan RMB

Where can I make a long distance call?
Wǒ dào nǎ er kě yǐ dǎ cháng tú diàn huà?
我 到 哪儿 可以 打 长 途 电 话？
I to go where might to make long distance phone call

I want to book a STD call to Shanghai/Canton.
Wǒ xiǎng yào Shàng hǎi/Guǎng dōng de cháng tú.
我 想 要 上 海/广 东 的 长 途。
I want to book Shanghai Canton long distance call

I want a person to person call to this person.
Wǒ yào dǎ gè jiào rén diàn huà.
我 要 打个 叫 人 电 话。
I want to make person to person phone call

The person you want is not there.
Nǐ yào zhǎo de rén bú zài.
你 要 找 的 人 不 在。
You want looking for person not there

The number you have dialed has changed. Please dial new number.
Nǐ bō de diàn huà hào mǎ yǐ gēng gǎi. Qǐng bō
你 拨 的 电 话 号 码 已 更 改。请 拨
You to dial telephone number already to change please dial

xīn hào mǎ.
新 号 码。
new number

The number you have dialed is not existing.
Nǐ bō de diàn huà hào mǎ bù cún zài.
你 拨 的 电 话 号 码 不 存 在。
You to dial telephone number not existing

Unable to get through the line. Please wait for some time.
Duì fāng xiàn lù máng, qǐng shāo hòu.
对 方 线 路 忙， 请 稍 候。
Other side line busy please wait some time

Where are you calling from?
Nǐ cóng ná er dǎ lái?
你 从 哪儿 打 来？
You from where call to come

Please cancel the call I have booked.
Qǐng qǔ xiāo wǒ yào de diàn huà.
请 取 消 我 要 的 电 话。
Please cancel I booked phone call

There is no reply from other side.

Duì fāng méi yǒu huí yìng.

对方 没有 回应。

Other side not have reply

The number you have dialed is wrong.

Nǐ bō cuò hào mǎ le.

你 拨 错 号码 了。

You to dial wrong number.

This telephone is out of order.

Zhè bù diàn huà huài le.

这部 电话 坏了。

This telephone out of order

A: Hello! This is paging service. Your name please?

Nǐ hǎo! Zhè li shì xún hū tái. Xiān shēng guì xìng?

你好！这里是 寻呼台。先生 贵姓？

Hello here is pager service sir good name

B: Mr. Kapur.

Kǎ pú er.

卡普尔。

Kapur

A: Your message please, sir.
Xiān shēng qǐng líu yán.
先 生 请 留 言
Sir please message

B: Please contact me immediately at phone number 66443322. This is urgent.
Qǐng jìn kuài yǔ wǒ lián xì, diàn huà shì
请 尽 快 与 我 联 系，电 话 是
Please immediately with me to contact telephone is

lìu lìu sì sì sān sān èr èr, yǒu jí shì.
六 六 四四 三 三 二 二，有 急 事。
6 6 4 4 3 3 2 2 have urgent matter

A: Anything else?
Hái yǒu ma?
还 有 吗？
Still have

B: No.
Méi le.
没 了。
No / finished

A: Please put down, sir.
Xiān shēng qǐng guà jī.
先 生 请 挂 机。
Sir please put down phone

Addl. Vocabulary

Telephone Exchange	*diàn huà jú*	电 话 局
Telephone Instrument	*diàn huà jī*	电 话 机
Telephone Operator	*jīe xiàn yuán*	接 线 员
Telephone Directory	*diàn huà bù*	电 话 簿
Telephone Bill	*diàn huà dān*	电 话 单
Extension Number	*fēn jī hào mǎ*	分 机 号 码
PBX	*xiǎo xíng jiāo huàn jī*	小 型 交 换 机
Digital Exchange	*shù zì jiāo huàn*	数 字 交 换
Cellular Phone	*shǒu jī*	手 机
Pager	*xún hū jī*	寻 呼 机
Public Telephone	*gōng yòng diàn huà*	公 用 电 话
Car Phone	*qì che diàn huà*	汽 车 电 话
Picture Phone	*diàn shì diàn huà*	电 视 电 话
Sim Card	*jiā mì kǎ*	加 密 卡
Phone Card	*diàn huà cí kǎ*	电 话 磁 卡

CHAPTER VI

Time And Date
Shí jiān hé rì qi
时 间 和 日 期

Time
Shí jiān
时 间

What time is it?
Jǐ diǎn le?
几 点 了？
What time

It is quarter to eleven.
Shí diǎn sì shí wǔ fēn / chā shí wǔ fēn shí yī diǎn.
十 点 四十五分 / 差 十 五 分 十一 点。
10.00 hrs 45 minutes less 15 minutes 11.00 hrs.

Excuse me, could you tell me the correct time?
Ní néng gào sù wǒ zhǔn què shí jiān ma?
你 能 告诉 我 准 确 时 间 吗？
You can to tell me correct time

My watch is fast / slow by 10 minutes.
Wǒ de biǎo kuài / màn shí fēn zhōng.
我 的 表 快 / 慢 十 分 钟。
My watch fast slow 10 minutes.

My watch has stopped.
Wǒ de biǎo tíng le.
我 的 表 停 了。
My watch stopped.

What time is it by your watch?
Nǐ de biāo jí diǎn le?
你 的 表 几 点 了？
Yours watch what time

It is ten o'clock sharp.
Shí diǎn zhèng.
十 点 正。
10.00 hrs sharp

Let me see. It's five minutes to eleven.
Ràng wǒ qiáo qiao. Xiàn zài shì shí yī diǎn chà wǔ fēn.
让 我 瞧 瞧。现 在 是 十 一 点 差 五 分。
Let me to check at present is 11.00hrs less 5 minutes

I think so. I set it by the radio / TV this morning.
Wǒ xiǎng shì de. Jīn tiān shàng wǔ wǒ cái duì guò
我 想 是的。今天 上 午 我 才 对 过
I to think yes today morning I only to correct

guǎng bō / diàn shì.
广 播 / 电 视。
radio TV

Does your watch give accurate time?
Nǐ de biǎo zǒu dé zhǔn ma?
你 的 表 走 的 准 吗？
Yours watch to move correct

It gains / loses about two minutes a day.
Tā měi tiān kuài / màn yuē liǎng fēn zhōng.
它 每 天 快 / 慢 约 两 分 钟。
It every day fast slow about 2 minutes

What is the time difference between India and China?
Yìn dù yǔ Zhōng guó de shí chā shì duō shǎo?
印 度 与 中 国 的 时 差 是 多 少？
India and China time difference is how much

China's time is ahead by two & half hours.
Zhōng guó bǐ Yìn dù zǎo liǎng gè bàn xiǎo shí.
中 国 比 印 度 早 两 个 半 小 时。
China than India ahead two and half hours

There is something wrong with my watch. I must have it repaired.
Wǒ de biǎo chū wèn tí le. Wǒ děi ná qù xīu yí xià.
我 的 表 出 问题了。我 得 拿 去 修 一下。
My watch to emerge problem I must take to go repair a while

I am sorry, I'm late.
Bào qiàn, wǒ chí dào le.
抱 歉，我 迟到 了。
Sorry I late

How long will it take?
Yào huā dūo shao shí jiān?
要 花 多 少 时 间？
Want spend how much time

What time will it end?
Shén me shí hòu cái jíe shù?
什 么 时后 才 结 束？
What time only to conclude

At what time should I be there?
Wǒ yīng gāi shén me shí hòu dáo?
我 应 该 什 么 时 候 到？
I should what time to reach

Can I come at 2:30 p.m.?
Wǒ xià wǔ liáng diǎn bàn dào, xíng ma?
我 下 午 两 点 半 到，行 吗？
I afternoon 2:30 hrs to reach all right

Date
rì qī
日期

What is the date today?
Jīn tiān jǐ hào le?
今天 几号 了？
Today what date

Today is 1 st September, 1997.
Jīn tiān shì yī jǐu jǐu qī nián jǐu yuè yī rì.
今天 是 一九九七 年 九月 一日。
Today is 1997 year September 1st

What was the date yesterday/day before yesterday?
Zuó tiān / qián tiān shì jǐ hào?
昨天 / 前天 是 几号？
Yesterday day before is what date

What will be the date tomorrow/day after tomorrow?
Míng tiān / hòu tiān shì jǐ hào?
明天 / 后天 是 几号？
Tomorrow day after is what date

When were you born?
Nǐ shì nǎ nián chū shēng de?
你 是 那 年 出生 的？
You are which year born

I was born in 1979.
Wǒ shì yī jǐu qī jǐu nián chū shēng de.
我 是 一九七九 年 出 生 的。
I was 1979 year born

What day is today?
Jīn tiān xīng qī jǐ le?
今天 星期几 了？
Today weekday what

Today is Sunday.
Jīn tiān xīng qī tiān.
今天 星期天。
Today Sunday

In India we work for five days in a week.
Zài Yìn dù wǒ men měi zhōu gōng zuò wǔ tiān.
在 印度 我们 每 周 工作 五 天。
At India we every week work five days

There is half an hour lunch time.
Wǔ fàn yǒu bàn gè xiǎo shí.
午饭 有 半个 小时。
Lunch have half hour

In China, we also work for five days a week.
Zài Zhōng guó, měi zhōu yě shì gōng zuò wǔ tiān.
在 中国，每 周 也 是 工作 五 天。
In China every week also is work 5 day

Our working hours are from 8:00 a.m. to 12:00 p.m. and from 2:00 p.m. to 6:00 p.m. in a day.

Wǒ men	*de*	*gōng zuò*	*shí jiān*	*shì*	*shàng wǔ*	*bā diǎn*
我们	的	工作	时间	是	上午	八点。
Our		work	time	is	morning	8:00 hrs

dào	*zhōng wǔ*	*shí èr diǎn,*	*xià wǔ*	*liǎng diǎn*	*dào*	*lìu diǎn.*
到	中午	十二点，	下午	两点	到	六点。
to	noon	12:00 hrs	afternoon	2:00 hrs	to	6:00 hrs

Addl. Vocabulary

Midnight	*wǔ yè*	午夜
Noon	*zhōng wǔ*	中午
Evening	*wǎn shang*	晚上
Seconds	*miǎo*	秒
Three days ago	*sān tiān yǐ qián*	三天以前
After two days	*liǎng tiān yǐ hòu*	两天以后
Week-end	*zhōu mò*	周末
Holiday	*jià rì*	假日

Week	*xīng qī*	星期
Month	*yuè*	月
Next day	*dì èr tiān*	第二天
Last month	*shàng gè yuè*	上个月
Next month	*xià gè yuè*	下个月
Next year	*lái nián*	来年
Last year	*qù nián*	去年
15th August 1947	*yī jǐu sì qī nián bā yuè shí wǔ rì*	一九四七年八月十五日
26th January 1950	*yī jǐu wǔ líng nián yī yuè èr shí lìu rì*	一九五零年一月二十六日

CHAPTER VII

Asking The Way
Wèn lù
问 路

A: Excuse me, could you tell me the way to railway station?
Duì bù qǐ, qǐng wèn dào huǒ chē zhàn zǒu nǎ tiáo lù?
对不起，请 问 到 火 车 站 走 哪 条 路？
Excuse me please tell to go railway station walk which road

B: You go right. After about 100 metres, take right turn and go straight.
Wǎng yòu, zǒu yì bái mǐ hòu zài wǎng yòu
往 右，走 一百 米 后 再 往 右
To right to walk 100 mts. then again to right

guǎi, rán hòu zhí zǒu jìu dào le.
拐，然 后 直 走 就 到 了。
to turn afterwards straight walk just reached

A: Is it far from here?
Lí zhè er yuǎn ma?
离 这 儿 远 吗？
From here far

B: It'snot far, only about 3 minutes walk.
Bú tài yuǎn, dà gài zǒu sān fēn zhōng.
不 太 远，大概 走 三 分 钟。
Not too far about to walk 3 minutes

A: Pardon me, could you tell me how to go to the airport?
Duì bù qǐ, qǐng wèn dào jī chǎng zěn me zǒu?
对 不起，请 问 到 机 场 怎 么 走？
Excuse me please tell to go airport how go

B: You can go to the nearest Airport Shuttle Service Stop or take a taxi.
Nǐ ké yǐ dào zuì jìn de mín háng bān chē zhàn
你 可以 到 最近 的 民 航 班 车 站
You may to go the nearest airlines shuttle stop

Huò zhe dǎ dī.
或 者 打的。
or take taxi

A: Excuse me, is there any post office nearby?
Qǐng wèn fù jìn yǒu yóu jú ma?
请 问 附近 有 邮 局 吗？
Please tell nearby have post office

B: Go straight. It's right on the main road.
Wǎng qiān zǒu, jìu zài dà lù biān shàng.
往 前 走，就 在 大路边 上。
To straight to walk just at main road side on

A: How far is Beijing University?

Dào Běi jīng dà xué yǒu duō yuǎn?

到 北京大学 有 多 远？

To Beijing University have how far

B: I am afraid you are going in a wrong direction.

Nǐ kě néng zǒu cuò fāng xiàng le.

你 可能 走 错 方向 了。

You perhaps to walk wrong direction

You go back and take left turn from the second red light.

Wǎng huí zǒu, dào di èr ge hōng dēng hòu

往 回 走，到 第二个 红 灯 后

Towards back to go up to the second red light after

zài zuǒ guǎi.

再 左 拐。

then left turn

A: Pardon me, Could you tell me the way to Indian Embassy?

Dǎ rǎo yí xià nǐ néng gào sù wǒ zěn yàng

打扰 一下，你 能 告诉 我 怎样

Pardon a while you can to tell me how

cái néng dào Yìn dù dà shí guǎn ma?

才能 到 印度 大使馆 吗？

only can reach Indian Embassy

B: Go straight from here.

Cóng zhè er yì zhí wǎng qián zǒu.

从 这儿 一直 往 前 走。

From here all along towards straight to walk

Turn right from the round about.

Dào dà yuán quān hòu wǎng yòu.

到 大圆圈 后 往 右。

Reach round about after to to right

From there, turn left from the first red light.

Yù dào dì yī gè hōng dēng zài wǎng zuǒ.

遇到 第一个 红灯 再 往 左。

Seeing the first red light then to left

After walking few paces, its on the other side of the road.

zǒu bù duō yuǎn, guò le mǎ lù jìu shì.

走 不 多 远，过 了 马路 就 是。

walk not much far crossed road that's it

A: Please tell me how to go to the Friendship Store?

Nǐ zhī dào Yǒu yì shāng diàn zěn me zǒu ma?

你 知道 友谊 上 店 怎么 走 吗？

You to know Friendship Store how to go

Should I get off the bus at the next stop?

Wǒ shì bú shì xià yí zhàn xià chē?

我 是不是 下一站 下车？

I whether or not the next stand down bus

Could you tell me where is the route no. 331 bus stop?
Láo jià, sān sān yāo lù chē zhàn zài nǎ er?
劳 驾， 三 三 一 路 车 站 在 哪 儿？
Excuse me 331 route bus stand at where

B: Turn right from next corner. After two blocks, It's there.
Dào xià yí gè lù kǒu xiàng yòu zhuǎn, zǒu
到 下 一 个 路 口 向 右 转， 走
Reach the next corner towards right to turn to go

guò liǎng gè jīe qū yǐ hòu jìu shì.
过 两 个 街 区 以 后 就 是。
pass two blocks after just is

A: Sorry for giving you trouble.
Dǎ rǎo nín le.
打 扰 您 了。
To disturb you

B: Not at all.
Bié kè qì.
别 客 气。
Not polite

Addl. Vocabulary

North	*běi*	北
South	*nán*	南
East	*dōng*	东
West	*xī*	西
Northeast	*dóng běi*	东 北
Northwest	*xī běi*	西 北
Southeast	*dōng nán*	东 南
Southwest	*xī nán*	西 南
Up / Above	*shàng biān/miàn*	上边/面
Down / Below	*xià biān/miàn*	下边/面
Ahead	*qián biān/miàn*	前边/面
Behind	*hòu biān/miàn*	后边/面
Middle	*zhōng jiān*	中 间
Opposite	*duì miàn*	对 面
Crossroads	*shí zì lù kǒu*	十 字 路 口
Pedestrian way	*rén xíng dào*	人 行 道
Zebra crossing	bān mǎ xiàn	斑 马 线
Fly over	*guò jīe tiān qiáo*	过 街 天 桥
Subway	*dì xià tōng dào*	地 下 通 道

CHAPTER VIII

Travelling By Bus/Metro
Gōng gòng qì chē / Dì tie
公 共 汽 车 / 地铁

A: Excuse me, where is the bus stop?
Qǐng wèn, gōng gòng qì chē zhàn zài nǎ er?
请 问，公 共 汽 车 站 在 哪 儿？
Please ask bus stand at where

B: Go straight and turn left / right, there is the bus terminal.
Zhí zǒu, rán hòu wǎng zuǒ / yòu guǎi jìu dào
直 走，然 后 往 左 / 右 拐 就 到
Straight walk, then to left right turn just to reach

shǐ fā zhàn le.
始 发 站 了。
terminal

A: I want to go to the Indian Embassy / Visa Office / Exhibition Centre.
Wǒ xiǎng qù Yìn dù dà shǐ guǎn / qiān zhèng chù/
我 想 去 印 度 大 使 管 / 签 政 处 /
I to think to go India embassy visa office

zhǎn lǎn zhōng xīn.
展 览 中 心。
exhibition centre

B: You take bus number 189 on the second / third ringroad.
Nǐ dào èr huán / sān huán zuò yāo bā jiǔ lù chē.
你到 二环 / 三 环 坐 一八九 路 车。
You to reach 2nd ring 3rd ring to sit 1 8 9 route bus

A: Where should I get down?
Wǒ dào nǎ er xià?
我 到 哪儿 下?
I to reach where to get off

B: You get down at....... You cross the road and take route number........
Nǐ dào..... xià, guò mǎ lù hòu zài shàng.... lù.
你到....下， 过 马路 后 再 上....路。
You to reach.... get down cross road then again to board... route

A: How much is the ticket?
Chē piào duō shao qián?
车票 多少 钱?
Bus ticket how much money

B: In the second ringroad, it is merely 5 jiao / mao.
Zài èr huán zhǐ yào wǔ jiǎo / máo qián.
在 儿环 只要 五角 / 毛 钱
At 2nd ring only five jiao mao money

In the third ringroad, it is 5 jiao/mao for every 5 stops.
Zài sān huán, měi wǔ zhān yào wǔ jiǎo/máo qián.
在 三 环，每 五 站 要 五 角 / 毛 钱。
At 3rd ring every 5 stand want 5 jiao / mao money

A: Is there any other way to go there?
Hái yǒu méi yǒu qí tā lù xiàn?
还 有 没 有 其 它 路 线？
Still have not have other route

B: You can also go by metro that will be much faster.
Nǐ hái kě yǐ chéng dì tiě, zhè yàng kuài de duō.
你 还 可以 乘 地铁，这 样 快 的 多。
You still may to board metro like this fast very

A: Is the metro station far from the bus stop?
Dì tiě zhàn lí gōng gòng qì chē zhàn yuǎn bù yuǎn?
地铁 站 离 公 共 汽 车 站 远 不 远？
Metro station from public bus stand far not far

B: No, in Beijing all the metro stations are near the bus stop.
Bù yuǎn, Běi jīng suǒ yǒu dì tiě zhàn dōu zài
不 远，北京 所 有 地铁 站 都 在
Not far Beijing all metro stations all at

gōng gòng qì chē zhàn fù jìn.
公 共 汽 车 站 附 近。
public bus stand near

A: How about metro ticket?
Dì tiě piào jià duō shao?
地铁 票 价 多 少?
Metro ticket rate how much

B: Not too expensive. It's only 2 yuan.
Yě bú gùi, zhǐ yào liǎng kuài qián.
也 不 贵，只 要 两 块 钱。
Also not costly only need two yuan money

A: What are the timings of metro?
Dì tiě shí jiān ne?
地铁 时 间 呢?
Metro time

B: It runs from 5:40 a.m. to 10:40 p.m. after every 5 minutes.
Cóng zǎo wǔ diǎn sì shí dào wǎn shí diǎn sì shí
从 早 五 点 四 十 到 晚 十 点 四 十
From morning 5 : 40 to evening 10 : 40

meǐ wǔ fēn zhong yǒu yí tàng.
每 五 分 钟 有 一 趟。
every 5 minutes have one trip

A: Thank you, I have bothered you so much.
Geǐ nín tiān má fán le.
给 您 添 麻 烦 了。
Give you to add trouble

B: Never mind, you are welcome.
Bié kè qì.
别 客 气。
Not polite

Addl. Vocabulary

Driver	*sī jī*	司 机
Conductor	*shòu piào yuán*	售 票 员
Ticket Counter	*shòu piào kǒu*	售 票 口
Ticket Checker	*jiàn piào yuán*	检 票 员
Escalator	*zì dòng fú tī*	自 动 扶 梯
Double Decker Bus	*shuāng céng kè chē*	双 层 客 车
Monthly Pass	*yuè piào*	月 票
Ring Metro	*huán xiàn dì tiě*	环 线 地 铁
No. 1 Metro	*yī xiàn dì tiě*	一 线 地 铁
Fly over	*lì jiāo qiáo*	立 交 桥
Over bridge	*rén xíng tiān qiáo*	人 行 天 桥

CHAPTER IX

Buying A Train Ticket
Mǎi huǒ chē piào
买 火 车 票

A: I want a train ticket to Shanghai.
Wǒ yào yì zhāng qù Shàng hǎi de huǒ chē piào.
我 要 一张 去 上 海 的 火 车 票。
I want one to go Shanghai train ticket

B: For which train?
Nǎ yí bān huǒ chē?
哪 一 班 火 车？
Which train

A: Oh, I don't know, but I think an afternoon train is the best.
Ó, wǒ bù zhī dào. Zuì hǎo shì xià wǔ de.
哦，我 不 知道。最 好 是 下 午 的。
Oh I not to know the best is afternoon

B: When do you want to go?
Nǐ xiǎng nǎ tiān zǒu?
你 想 哪 天 走？
You to think which day to go

A: I want to go by tomorrow'strain.
Wǒ xiǎng míng tiān bān chē zou.
我 想 明 天 班 车 走。
I to think tomorrow train to go

B: Which ticket do you want to buy?
Nín mǎi nǎ zhǒng piào?
你 买 哪 种 票？
You to buy which type ticket

A: I want to buy a sleeper ticket.
Wǒ yào wò pū piào.
我 要 卧 铺 票。
I want sleeper ticket

B: Soft sleeper or hard sleeper?
Ruǎn wò hǎi shì yìng wò?
软 卧 还 是 硬 卧？
Soft sleeper or hard sleeper

A: I would prefer air-conditioned soft sleeper.
Zuì hǎo shì yǒu kōng tiáo de ruǎn wò.
最 好 是 有 空 调 的 软 卧。
The best is have air-condition soft sleeper

B: Sorry! Both are not available. Only hard seats are there.
Duì bù qǐ! Ruǎn, yìng wò dōu méi yǒu le. Zhǐ yǒu yìng zuò.
对不起！软，硬我 都 没有了。只有 硬座。
Sorry soft hard sleeper all don't have only have hard seat

A: Then I will buy a hard seat.
Nà wǒ mǎi yìng zuò.
那 我 买 硬 座。
Then I buy hard seat

What is the train number?
Huǒ chē cì shì dūo shao?
火 车 次 是 多 少？
Train no is how much

B: Train number is 21.
Huǒ chē hào ma shì èr shí yī.
火 车 号 码 是 二 十 一。
Train no. is twenty one

A: How much is for one ticket?
Duō shao qián yì zhāng piào?
多 少 钱 一 张 票？
How much money one ticket

B: It is 120 yuan.
Yī bǎi èr shí kuài qián.
一百二十 块 钱。
1 2 0 yuan money

A: At what time does the train leave?
Huǒ chē shén me shí hòu kāi?
火车 什么 时候 开？
Train what time start

B: The train leaves at 3:15 p.m.
Huǒ chē xià wǔ sān diǎn yí kè kāi.
火车 下午 三点一刻 开。
Train afternoon 3:15 start

A: From which station does the train start?
Cóng nǎ gè chē zhàn fā chē?
从 哪个 车站 发车？
From which station start train

B: The train starts from Beijing Western Railway station.
Cóng běi jīng xī kè zhàn fā chē.
从 北京 西客站 发车。
From Beijing west station start train

A: Is Beijing Western Railway station far from Beijing Railway Station?

Běi jīng xī kè zhàn lí Běi jīng zhàn yuǎn ma?

北京 西客站 离 北京 站 远 吗？

Beijing west station from Beijing station far

B: Not too far, there is a shuttle between the two stations.

Bú tài yuǎn. Liǎng zhàn zhī jiān yǒu yí tàng

不 太 远。 两 站 之间 有 一趟

Not too far two station between have one

zhí tōng chē.

直 通 车。

direct train

Addl. Vocabulary

Platform	*yuè tái*	月台
Waiting Room	*hòu chē shì*	候车室
Dining Car	*cān chē*	餐车
Train Attendant	*liè chē fú wù yuán*	列车服务员
Bedding	*wò jù*	卧具

Upper Berth	*shàng pū*	上 铺
Lower Berth	*xià pū*	下 铺
Hot Water	*kāi shuǐ*	开 水
Passenger Train	*pǔ kuài*	普 快
Express Train	*zhí kuài*	直 快
Superfast	*tè kuài*	特 快
Goods Train	*huò wù liè chē*	货 物 列 车
Engine	*huǒ chē tóu*	火 车 头

CHAPTER X

At the Bank
Zài yín háng
在 银 行

A: I want to deposit one thousand US $ in current account.
Wǒ xiǎng cún yì qīan měi yuán huó qī.
我 想 存 一千 美元 活期。
I think deposit 1000 US$ current account

B: Please fill in your name and amount in the deposit slip.
Qǐng zài cún kuǎn dān shàng tián xǐe nǐ de
请 在 存款单 上 填写 你的
Please at deposit slip on to write you

míng zì hé cún kuǎn shù é.
名字 和 存款 数额。
name and deposit amount

A: What is the interest rate?
Lì xī shì duō shao?
利息 是 多少？
Interest is how much

B: Interest rate is 4%.
Lì xī shì bǎi fēn zhī sì.
利息 是 百 分 之 四。
Interest is percent four

A: What about one year fixed deposit?
Cún yì nián de dìng qī lì xī shì duō shao?
存 一年 的 定 期 利 息 是 多 少？
Deposit one year fixed term interest is how much

B: It is 14% per annum.
Yì nián de lì xī shì bǎi fēn zhī shí sì.
一年 的 利息 是 百 分 之 十 四。
One year interest is percent 14

A: Can I withdraw the fixed deposit in advance?
Wǒ néng bù néng tí qián qǔ chū dìng qī cún kuǎn?
我 能 不能 提前 取出 定期 存 款？
I can not can ahead withdraw fixed term deposit money

B: Yes, you can. Then the interest rate will be the same as for the current account.
Kě yǐ. Dàn dào shí lì xī yǔ huó qī yí yàng le.
可以。但 到 时 利息 与 活期 一样 了。
Can but expiry date interest with current same

A: What if I lose my passbook?

Rù guǒ wǒ dīu le cún zhé zěn me bàn?

如果 我 丢 了 存折 怎么 办？

If I lost deposit slip what to do

B: You should report the loss to the bank immediately.

Nǐ bì xū lì kè xiàng yín háng guà shī.

你 必须 立刻 向 银行 挂失。

You must immediately towards bank report loss

A: Would you also please encash this cheque for 200 pounds?

Nǐ néng duì huàn zhè zhāng èr bǎi yīng bàng

你 能 兑换 这 张 二百 英镑

You can to exchange this 200 pounds

de zhī piào ma?

的 支票 吗？

cheque

You please got to the last counter.

Qǐng dào zuì hòu yí gè guì tái.

请 到 最后 一个 柜台。

Please to reach last one counter

B: Can you change this in to Ren min bi (RMB).

Nǐ néng bǎ tā huàn chéng Rén mín bì ma?

你 能 把 它 换 成 人民币 吗？

You can let it change into RMB

What is the exchange rate?
Duì huàn lǜ shì duō shao?
兑 换 率 是 多 少？
Exchange rate is how much

B: It is...... RMB for 100 pounds.
Duì huàn lǜ shì yī bǎi yīng bàng.... Rén mín bì.
兑 换 率 是 一百 英 镑 ....人 民 币。
Exchange rate is 100 Pounds... RMB

Addl. Vocabulary

People's Bank of China
Zhōng guó rén mín yín háng
中 国 人民 银 行

Industry & Commerce Bank
Gōng shāng yín háng
工 商 银 行

Construction Bank
Jiàn shè yín háng
建 设 银 行

Exim Bank
Jìn chū kǒu yín háng
进 出 口 银 行

Agricultural Bank
Nóng yè yín háng
农 业 银 行

Bank Manager
yín háng jīng lǐ
银 行 经 理

Cashier / Teller
chū nà yuán
出 纳 员

Account Number
cūn dān hào
存 单 号

Cheque Book
zhī piào bù
支 票 簿

Balance
jíe yú
结 余

Withdrawal Slip
qǔ kuǎn dān
取 款 单

Deposit Slip
cūn kuǎn dān
存 款 单

ATM
zì dòng tí kuǎn jī
自 动 提 款 机

Travellers Cheque
lǚ xíng zhī piào
旅 行 支 票

Credit Card
xìn yòng kǎ
信 用 卡

Bonds
zhài quàn
债 券

Loan
dài kuǎn
贷 款

Bank Draft
huì piào
汇 票

Currency
Huò bì
货 币

U.S.Dollar
Meǐ yuán
美 元

Pound Sterling
Yīng bàng
英 镑

Rouble
Lú bù
卢 布

Japanese Yen
Rì yuán
日 元

Rupee
Lú bǐ
卢 比

German Mark
Mǎ kè
马 克

French Franc
Fǎ láng
法 郎

Hong Kong Dollar
Gǎng bì
港 币

CHAPTER XI

At The Post Office
Zài yóu jú
在 邮局

A: At what time does the post office open / close?
Yóu jú jǐ diǎn kāi mén / guān mén?
邮局 几点 开门 / 关门?
Post office what time open gate close gate

B: The post office opens from 8 a.m. to 5 p.m.
Yóu jú zǎo bā diǎn kāi mén, dào xìa wǔ
邮局 早 八点 开门, 到 下午
Post office morning 8:00hrs open gate up to afternoon

wǔ diǎn guān mén.
五点 关门。
5:00hrs close gate

A: How much does it cost to mail a letter inside China?
Fā yì fēng píng xìn yào mǎi duō shǎo qián
发 一封 平信 要 买 多 少 钱
To post one ord. letter want buy how much money

de yóu piào?
的 邮票?
postal stamp

B: It costs 5 jiao / mao.

Zhǐ yào wǔ jiǎo / máo.

只要 五角 / 毛。

Only need 5 jiao mao

A: What is the postage for a letter to India?

Jì yí fēng xìn dào Yìn dù yào duō shao qián?

寄一封 信到 印度 要 多少 钱?

Mail one letter to reach India want how much money

B: It is 6.5 yuan.

Lìu kuài wǔ máo qián.

六块 五毛 钱。

Six yuan five mao money

A: How many days will it take to reach?

Yào duō shao tiān cái néng jì dào?

要 多少 天 才能 寄到?

Want how much day only can to mail to reach

B: It will take seven to ten days.

Qī dào shí tián.

七到 十 天。

Seven to ten days

A: If I want to send through EMS, how much will be the postage?
Rù guǒ wǒ fā tè kuài zhuān dì, yóu fèi shì
如果 我 发 特快 专递，邮 费 是
If I to dispatch express service postal charge is

duō shao?
多 少？
how much

B: Minimum charges for EMS are 120 yuan.
Zhì shǎo yī bǎi èr shí kuài Rén mín bì.
至少 一百二十 块 人民 币。
Minimum 120 yuan RMB

A: How much is the postage for sending a parcel to India?
Jì yí gè bāo guǒ dào Yìn dù yào duō shao?
寄 一个 包 裹 到 印度 要 多 少？
Mail one packet up to India want how much

B: Do you want to send it by airmail or by ship?
Nǐ xiǎng yào háng kōng yóu jì hái shì
你 想 要 航 空 邮 寄 还 是
You to think want by air to post or

pǔ tōng yóu jì?
普 通 邮 寄？
ordinary to post

A: I want to send it by airmail.
Háng kōng yóu jì.
航空 邮寄。
By air to post

B: It is 200 yuan up to 500 grams.
Wǔ bǎi kè yǐ xià yào liǎng bǎi kuài qián.
五百 克 以下 要 两百 块 钱。
500 gms below want 200 yuan money

A: What are the domestic rates for parcels?
Guó nèi jì bāo guǒ yào duō shao qián?
国内 寄 包裹 要 多少 钱?
Domestic to mail packet want how much money

B: It is 30 yuan up to 500 grams.
Wǔ bǎi kè yǐ xià yào sān shí kuài qián.
五百 克 以下 要 三十 块 钱。
500 gms below want 30 yuan money

A: I want to buy some commemorative stamps.
Wǒ hái xiǎng mǎi xīe jì niàn yóu piào.
我 还 想 买 些 纪念 邮票。
I also to think to buy some commemorate postage stamps

B: You please go to the next counter.
Qǐng dào xià yí gè guì tái.
请 到 下一个 柜台。
Please to the next one counter

A: Where is the mail box?
Xìn xiāng zài nǎ er?
信 箱 在 哪儿？
Letter box at where

B: It is outside the post office.
Jìu zài yóu jú mén wài.
就 在 邮局 门 外。
Just at post office outside the gate

Addl. Vocabulary

Postage Stamps	*yóu piào*	邮票
Postcard	*míng xìn piàn*	明信片
Money Order	*huì kuǎn dān*	汇款单
Acknowledgement	*cún gēn*	存根
Aerogramme	*háng kōng xìn*	航空信
Printed Matter	*yìn shuā pǐn*	印刷品
Address	*dì zhǐ*	地址

Post Code	yóu zhèng biān mǎ	邮 政 编 码
Envelope	*xìn fēng*	信 封
Telegram	*diàn bào*	电 报
Telex	*diàn chuán*	电 传
STD	*guó nèi cháng tú diàn huà*	国 内 长 途 电 话
ISD	*guó jì cháng tú diàn huà*	国 际 长 途 电 话

CHAPTER XII

See A Doctor
Kàn bìng
看 病

A: I want to see a doctor.
Wǒ yào kàn bìng.
我 要 看 病。
I want to see a doctor

Is there any clinic nearby?
Fù jìn yǒu zhén suǒ ma?
附近 有 诊所 吗?
Nearby have clinic

Can you call a doctor for me?
Nǐ néng bāng wǒ jiào yī shēng ma?
你 能 帮 我 叫 医生 吗?
You can to help me to call doctor

I am not feeling well.
Wǒ bú tài shū fu.
我 不 太 舒服。
I not too comfortable

B: What's wrong with you?
Nǐ zěn me bù shū fu a?
你 怎 么 不 舒 服 啊？
You how not comfortable

A: I have a headache, sore throat and cough.
Wǒ tóu téng, hóu lóng téng, ké sòu.
我 头 痛，喉 咙 疼，咳 嗽。
I headache sore throat cough

I have some problem with my eyes.
Wǒ yǎn jīng yǒu diǎn wèn tí.
我 眼 睛 有 点 问 题。
I eyes have little problem

I have diarrhea and sensation of vomiting.
Wǒ lā dù zi, hái yǒu diǎn xiǎng tù.
我 拉 肚 子，还 有 点 想 吐。
I upset stomach also have little to feel to vomit

B: Let me examine you first.
Xiān ràng wǒ jiǎn chá yí xià.
先 让 我 检 查 一 下。
First let me to check a while

Please lie down here.
Qǐng tǎng zài zhè er.
请 躺 在 这 儿。
Please lie down at here

How long have you been feeling like this?
Xiàng zhè yàng yǒu duō jǐu le?
像 这 样 有 多 久 了?
Like this type have how long

A: Since yesterday I am feeling uncomfortable.
Cóng zuó tiān qǐ jìu yǒu xīe bù shū fu.
从 昨 天 起 就 有 些 不 舒 服。
From Yesterday onwards have some not comfortable

B: Open your mouth.
Zhāng zuǐ.
张 嘴。
Open mouth

Take a deep breath.
Shēn hū xī.
深 呼 吸。
Deep breath

Cough please.
Kè yí xià.
咳 一下。
Cough a while

Let me check your temperature and blood pressure.
Wǒ lái chá yí xià nǐ de tǐ wēn hé xué yā.
我 来 查 一下 你 的 体温 和 血 压。
I come to check a while your body temp. and blood pressure

Is this the first time you have this problem?
Nǐ dì yī cì gǎn jué zhè yàng ma?
你 第一次 感 觉 这 样 吗？
You first time feeling this type

A: No, I often have this problem.
Bù, wǒ jīng cháng zhè yàng.
不，我 经 常 这 样。
Not I often this type

B: Your temperature is 39 degrees. You have fever.
Nǐ de tǐ wēn yǒu sān shí jiǔ dù. Nǐ fā shāo le.
你的 体温 有 三 十 九 度。你 发 烧 了。
Your body temp. have thirty nine degrees you fever

You should take bed rest for few days.
Nǐ zùi hǎo wò chuáng xīu xi jǐ tiān.
你 最好 卧 床 休息 几 天。
You the best bed to rest few days

A: Is there anything serious, doctor?
Wèn tí yán zhòng ma, yī shēng?
问 题 严 重 吗，医 生？
Problem serious doctor

B: There is nothing serious. You have cold/food poisoning.
Méi yǒu shén me yán zhòng wèn tí. Nǐ gǎn mào/
没 有 什 么 严 重 问 题。你 感 冒/
No what serious problem you cold

shí wù zhòng dú le.
食 物 中 毒 了。
food poison

You have over-exerted yourself.
Nǐ guò dù láo lèi le.
你 过度 劳 累 了。
You over exerted

I will give you injection and some medicines.
Wǒ gěi nǐ dǎ yì zhēn, zài gěi nì yī xiē yào.
我 给 你 打 一针，再 给 你 一些 药。
I to give one injection and give you some medicine

Please take these pills three times a day.
Zhè xìe yào yì tiān chī sān cì.
这些 药 一天 吃 三次。
Some medicine one day eat 3 times.

Two yellow, one red pill in the morning before meals.
Zǎo fàn qián fú liǎng piàn huáng sè, yí piàn
早饭 前 服 两片 黄色，一片
Breakfast before take 2 pills yellow one pill

hóng sè de yào.
红色 的 药。
red medicine

One red, one green in the afternoon after meals.
Xìa wǔ yí piàn hóng sè, yí piàn lǜ sè.
下午 一片 红色，一片 绿色。
Afternoon one pill red one pill green

One red, two yellow pills before going to bed.
Shuì qián yí piàn hóng sè, liǎng piàn huáng sè.
睡前 一片 红色，两片 黄色。
Sleep before one pill red two pills yellow

Take these medicines along with hot water.
Dōu yòng kāi shuǐ chōng fú.
都 用 开水 冲服。
All to use hot water to take

Take one spoon of this syrup whenever you feel feverish.
Júe de fā shāo le jìu fú yòng yì sháo táng jiàng.
觉 得 发烧 了 就 服用 一勺 糖 浆。
To feel fever then to take one spoon syrup

Shake well before using it. Report after seven days.
Shǐ yòng qián yào yáo dòng. Qī tiān yǐ hòu
使 用 前 要 摇 动。 七 天 以 后
Using before need to shake 7 days after

zài lái fù zhěn.
再 来 复 诊。
again come to consult

A: How much is the fees?
Yào fèi yǒu duō shao?
药 费 有 多 少？
Med.charge have how much

B: It's 160 yuan. Please pay it at the cash counter.
Yī bǎi liù shí yuán. Qǐng dào shōu fèi chù
一百 六 十 元。 请 到 收 费 处
1 6 0 yuan please reach cash counter

jiāo qián.
交 钱。
to handover money

A: Thanks for your help, doctor.
Xìe xìe nín, yī shēng.
谢谢 您，医生。
Thank you doctor

Addl. Vocabulary

Registration Counter	*guà hào shì*	挂号室
Emergency	*jí zhěn shì*	急诊室
Ward	*zhù yuàn bù*	住院部
O.P.D.	*mén zhěn bù*	门诊部
Surgeon	*wài kē yī shēng*	外科医生
Nurse	*hù shì*	护士
Surgery	*wài kē shōu shù*	外科手术
Ambulance	*jí jìu chē*	急救车
Thermometer	*wēn dù jì*	温度计
Bandage	*bāo zhā*	包扎
Ultra Sound	*B-chāo*	B-超
Cat Scan	*C T*	C T
X-ray	*X-guāng*	X-光

Anesthesia	*má zuì*	麻 醉
Intravenous Fluid	*shū yè*	输 液
Blood Transfusion	*shū xuě*	输 血
Blood Bank	*xuě kù*	血 库
Blood Group	*xuě xíng*	血 型
Acupuncture	*zhēn jīu*	针 灸
Massage	*àn mó*	按 摩
Dentist	*yá kē yī shēng*	牙 科 医 生
E.N.T. Specialist	*ěr bí hóu yī shēng*	耳 鼻 喉 医 生
Gynaecologist	*fù kē yī shēng*	妇 科 医 生
Paediatrician	*ér kē yī shēng*	儿 科 医 生
Fracture	*gǔ zhé*	骨 折
Swelling	*fā yán*	发 炎
Acidity	*wèi suān*	胃 酸
Asthma	*qì chuǎn*	气 喘
Sun-stroke	*zhòng shǔ*	中 署
Cramps	*chōu jīn*	抽 筋

Heart Disease	*xīn zàng bìng*	心脏病
Backache	*bèi tòng*	背痛
Rheumatism	*fēng shī*	风湿
Ulcer	*kuì yáng*	溃疡
Burn	*shāo shāng*	烧伤
Jaundice	*gān yán*	肝炎
Pneumonia	*fèi yán*	肺炎
Gall-stone	*dān jíe shí*	胆结石
Skin Disease	*pí fū bìng*	皮肤病
Appendictis	*lān wěi yán*	阑尾炎
Diabetes	*táng niào bǐng*	糖尿病
Acute Disease	*jí xìng bìng*	急性病
Chronic Disease	*màn xìng bìng*	慢性病
Infection	*chuán rǎn bìng*	传染病
Wheelchair	*lún yǐ*	轮椅
Western Medicine	*xī yī*	西医
Chinese Medicine	*zhōng yī*	中医
Herbal Medicine	*cǎo yào*	草药

CHAPTER XIII

At The Barber's
Zài lǐ fà
在 理 发

A: Please give me a hair cut.
Wǒ yào lǐ fà.
我 要 理发。
I want hair cut

B: How would you like your hair done sir?
Ní xiǎng yào lǐ shèn me yàng de, xiān sheng?
你 想 要 理 什 么 样 的，先 生？
You like want to remove what style Mr./sir

A: Not too long on the back. Just a trim on the sides.
Use scissors only, no clippers.
Hòu miàn bú yào jiǎn tài cháng. Liǎng biān bú yào
后 面 不 要 剪 太 长。两 边 不 要
Rear side not want to cut too long two sides not want

jiǎn tài duō. Zhǐ yòng jiǎn dāo, bú yào yòng tuī zi.
剪 太 多。只 用 剪 刀，不 要 用 推子。
to cut too much only use scissors not want use clipper

B: Is it all right?

Zhè yàng xíng ma?

这 样 行 吗？

This type O.K.

A: Take a little more off on the top and sides.

Tóu dǐng hé lǐang biān zài duō jiǎn diǎn.

头顶 和 两 边 再 多 剪 点。

On the top and two sides again more to cut a bit

B: Would you like to shampoo your hair, sir?

Ní xiǎng xǐ tóu ma?

你 想 洗 头 吗？

You like wash head

A: Yes. I also want my shave done.

Xǐ tóu. Zài xīu xīu miàn.

洗 头。再 修修 面。

Wash head then to shave face

Please trim my mustaches.

Qǐng bá wǒ de hú zi xiū jiǎn.

请 把 我 的 胡子 修 剪。

Please let my mustaches to trim

Please dye my hair black.
Qǐng bá wǒ de tóu fà rǎn chéng hēi sè.
请 把 我 的 头发 染 成 黑色。
Please let my hair to dye to become black

That's fine.
Tài bàng le.
太 棒 了。
Too good

Addl. Vocabulary

Facial	*miàn fū*	**面 敷**
Hair Set	*fà xíng*	**发 型**
After Shave Lotion	*xīu miàn xiāng yè*	**修 面 香 液**
Bald	*guāng tóu*	**光 头**
Wig	*jiǎ fà*	**假 发**
Dandruff	*tóu xǜe*	**头 屑**
Curly Hair	*juǎn fà*	**卷 发**

Razor	*guā hú dāo*	刮胡刀
Blade	*dāo piàn*	刀片
Hair Drier	*chūi fēng jī*	吹风机
Shaving Cream	*xīu miàn gāo*	修面膏
Shaving Brush	*xīu miàn shuā*	修面刷

CHAPTER XIV

Talking About The Weather
Tán lùn Tiān qì
谈 论 天 气

A: Did you see the weather forecast on TV yesterday?
Zuó tiān nǐ kàn diàn shì shàng de
昨 天 你 看 电 是 上 的
Yesterday you to see TV on

tiān qì yù bào le ma?
天 气 预 报 了 吗？
weather forecast

B: Yes. I saw it after the evening news.
Kàn le. Wǒ shì zài wǎn jiān xīn wén hòu kàn de.
看 了。我 是 在 晚 间 新 闻 后 看 的。
Saw I am at evening news after to see

A: How will be the weather today?
Jīn tiān tiān qì rù hé?
今 天 天 气 如 何？
Today weather how

B: According to the forecast, it will be clear in the morning but become cloudy later in the day.
Gēn jù yù bào , shàng wǔ qíng tiān yǐ hòu
根据 预报，上 午 晴 天 以后
As per forecast morning clear day after

qíng zhuǎn duō yún.
晴 转 多 云。
clear to change cloudy

A· Is there any likelihood of rain?
Huì bú huì xià yǔ?
会不会 下 雨？
Whether or not fall rain

B: There might be thunder-shower in the evening.
Bàng wǎn ké néng yǒu léi zhèn yǔ.
傍 晚 可能 有 雷阵 雨。
Towards evening may have thunder shower

A: What will be the temperature during the daytime?
Bái tiān qì wen duo shao?
白天 气温 多 少？
Day time temperature how much

B: It will be around 26 degree.
Dà yuē èr shí lìu shè shì dù.
大约 二十六 摄氏度。
About twenty six degree C

A: Will it be windy also?
Yǒu fēng ma?
有 风 吗?
Have wind

B: There might be winds ranging from force 2 to 3.
Yǒu, fēng lì yuē èr dào sān jí.
有，风力 约 二 到 三 级。
Yes wind force about two to three level

A: Is the weather forecast reliable?
Tiān qì yù bào zhun bù zhun què?
天气预报 准 不 准 确?
weather forecast accurate not accurate

B: Most of the time the weather forecast is accurate.
Dà duō shù tiān qì yù bào dōu shì zhun què de.
大多数 天气预报 都 是 准 确 的。
Mostly weather forecast all are accurate

A: Could you tell me about the climatic conditions of Beijing?
Nǐ néng tán tan Běi jīng de tiān qì qíng kuàng ma?
你能 谈谈 北京 的 天气 情 况 吗?
You can to discuss Beijing weather condition

B: Is it your first trip to Beijing?
Nǐ shì dì yī cì dào Běi jīng ma?
你 是 第一次 到 北京 吗？
You are the first to reach Beijing

A: Yes, and I don't know much about the climate here.
Shì de. Wǒ hái bú tài liáo jiě zhè lǐ de tiān qì.
是的。我 还 不 太 了解 这里 的 天 气。
Yes I still not too understand here weather

B: Beijing have four seasons: spring, summer, autumn, winter.
Běi jīng yǒu sì jì: Chūn , Xià, Qīu, Dōng.
北京 有 四季： 春 ，夏，秋， 冬。
Beijing have four seasons spring summer autumn winter

A: Is it very hot here?
Zhè li shì bú shì hěn rè?
这里 是不是 很 热？
Here whether or not very hot

B: No. The temperature in summers remains below 35 degree.
Bú rè. Xià tiān bú huì chāo guò sān shí wǔ shè shì dù.
不热。夏天 不会 超过 三十五 摄氏度。
Not hot summer cannot to cross thirty five degree C

A: When does the summers start here?
Zhè li xià tiān shén me shí hòu kāi shi?
这里 夏天 什么 时候 开始？
Here summer what time to start

A: The summer season is from June to August.
Lìu dàc bā yuè dōu shì xià tiān.
六 到 八月 都 是 夏天。
June to August all are summer

A: It doesn't seems to be very hot.
Hǎo xiàng bú shì tài rè.
好 像 不 是 太 热。
Looks like not is too hot

B: Yes. But the winters here are very cold.
Duì. Dàn zhè er de dōng tiān hén lěng.
对。但 这 儿 的 冬 天 很 冷。
Yes but here winter very cold

A: Really? How cold is it?
Shì ma? Yǒu duó lěng?
是 吗？有 多 冷？
Is it so have how cold

B: During winters, the day temperature is around -2 to -3 °C
Dào dōng tiān, bái tiān de qì wēn dōu zài
到 冬 天，白 天 的 气 温 都 在
To reach winter day time temperature all at

líng xià èr dào sān shè shì dù.
零 下 二 到 三 摄 氏 度。
zero below two to three degree C

A: What about night?
Nà me wǎn shang ne?
那么 晚上 呢？
Then evening

B: The night temperature sometimes reaches to -20ºC.
Wǎn shang yǒu shí huì jiàng dào líng xià èr shí
晚上 有时 会 降到 零下 二十
Evening sometimes can to reduce to zero below twenty

shè shì dù.
摄氏度。
degree C

A: It must be very cold. Then how do people survive?
Zhè yě tài lěng le. Zěn me cái néng áo guò qù a?
这 也 太 冷 了。怎么 才能 熬过去啊？
This also too cold how only can survive

B: Most of the buildings here are centrally heated. Inside it's very nice and warm.
Yì bān dà lóu lǐ miàn dōu yǒu nuǎn qì.
一般 大 楼 里面 都 有 暖气。
Generally big building inside all have central heating

Dāi zài lǐ miàn hěn shū fu.
待 在 里面 很 舒服。
stay at inside very comfortable

When people go out, they wear padded and warm clothes.
Zhí yǒu chū mén de shí hòu caí chuān hòu yī fu.
只有 出门 的 时后 才 穿 厚 衣服。
Only to go out point of time only to wear padded cloths

A: Does it snow here?
Zhè er hái xià xuě ma?
这 儿 还 下 雪 吗？
Here also to fall snow

B: Yes, it does. You have to protect yourself carefully against the chilly winds.
Dāng rán xià. Ní děi xiǎo xīn bié ràng hán fēng
当 然 下。你 得 小 心 别 让 寒 风
Of course to fall you must careful not let cold wind

chuī zhāo le.
吹 著 了。
to blow up

A: Which is the best season here?
Zhè li zuì hǎo de jì jié shì shén me shí hòu?
这 里 最 好 的 季 节 是 什 么 时 候？
Here the best season is what time

B: Autumns are the best. During this season, the weather is very fine.
Qīu tiān zuì hǎo. Nà gè shí hòu de tiān qì zuì yí rén.
秋天 最好。那个 时候 的 天气 最怡人。
Autumn the best that point of time weather the most joyful

A: Which is the autumn peroid?
shén me shí hòu shì Qīu tiān?
什么 时候 是 秋天？
What point of time is autumn

B: It's from September to November.
Cóng jǐu yuè dào shí yī yuè.
从 九月 到 十一月。
From September to November

A: How about the weather in springs?
Nà chūn tiān zěn me yàng ā?
那 春天 怎么样 啊？
Then spring how

B: It is very comfortable during spring. It's green all over and many people enjoy their evenings in public parks.
Chūn tiān yé hěn shū fu. Dào chù dōu lǜ le, gōng yuán
春天 也 很 舒服。到处 都 绿了，公园
Spring also very nice every where all green garden

li lián wǎn shang dōu yǒu hěn duō rén.
里 连 晚上 都 有 很多 人。
in even evening all have many persons

B: Thank you for your valuable information.
Xìe xìe nǐ gào sù wǒ zhè xiē xiāo xi.
谢谢 你 告诉 我 这些 消息。
Thank you to tell me these information

A: It's my pleasure.
Bié kè qì.
别 客 气。
Not polite

Addl. Vocabulary

Lightning	*shǎn diàn*	**闪电**
Hailstorm	*bīng bào*	**冰雹**
Duststorm	*shā bào*	**沙暴**
Dewdrops	*lù shui*	**露水**
North-West winds	*xī běi fēng*	**西北风**
Dark-clouds	*wū yún*	**乌云**
Blue sky	*lán tiān*	**蓝天**

Sun Shine	*yáng guāng*	阳光
Moon Light	*yuè guāng*	月光
Drizzling	*xiáo yǔ*	小雨
Raincoat	*yǔ yī*	雨衣
Umbrella	*yǔ sǎn*	雨伞
Avalanche	*xuě bēng*	雪崩

CHAPTER XV

Sight-seeing
Lǚ yóu
旅 游

A: What are you doing this weekend?
Nǐ zhè gè zhōu mò yǒu shì ma?
你 这个 周 末 有 事 吗？
You this weekend have business

B: I am free.
Méi shì.
没 事。
No business.

A: Then lets go for sight-seeing in Beijing.
Nà wǒ men gùang Běi jīng qù.
那 我们 逛 北京 去。
Then we to roam around Beijing to go

B: This is a good idea. But how will we go?
Hǎo zhú yì. Zěn me qù ā?
好 主意。怎么 去 啊？
Good idea how to go

A: We will go in tourist bus. That is cheap and best.
Chèng lǚ yóu chē, jià lián wù měi.
乘 旅游 车，价 廉 物 美。
To board tourist bus cheap and the best

B: That's fine. Where to get tickets?
Tài bàng le. Dào ná er mǎi piào a?
太 棒 了。到 哪儿 买 票 啊？
Too good to reach where to buy ticket

A: We will buy tickets from tourist office.
Dào lǚ xíng shè mǎi.
到 旅行 社 买。
To reach travel agency to buy

B: At what time does the city tour starts?
Chē jí diǎn zhōng kāi?
车 几点 钟 开？
Bus what time to start

A: I think at 9.00 o'clock in the morning. But we will reconfirm it from tourist office.
Wǒ xiǎng shì zǎo shang jíu diǎn ba. Děng dào
我 想 是 早 上 九 点 吧。等 到
I to think is morning 9:00 a.m. to wait to reach

lǚ xíng shè zài hé shí yí xià.
旅行 社 再 核实 一 下。
tourist agency then verify a while

B: Does the ticket include entry fee also?

Chē piào qián hán mén piào ma?

车 票 钱 含 门 票 吗？

Bus ticket money include gate ticket

A: No, we have to purchase entry tickets by ourselves.

Bù hán. Wǒ men děi zì jǐ mǎi mén piào.

不 含。我 们 得 自己 买 门 票。

Not to include we must ourselves buy gate ticket

Where are we going first?

Wǒ men xiān qù nǎ er?

我 们 先 去 哪 儿？

We first to go where

B: We are going to a place called Badaling to see the Great Wall of China.

Xiān dào Bā dá lǐng, kàn Cháng chéng qù.

先 到 八达岭，看 长 城 去。

First to reach Badaling to see Great Wall to go

A: Is this the only spot to see the Great Wall in Beijing?

Nà er shì Běi jīng wéi yī ké yǐ kàn Cháng chéng

那儿 是 北 京 唯一 可以看 长 城

There is Beijing only may to see Great Wall

de dì fāng ma?

的 地方 吗？

place

B: No, there are other spots also. But you can have best view of the Great Wall from there.
Bù zhǐ, hái yǒu háo jǐ gè dì fāng. Dàn nà er de
不止，还有 好 几个 地方。但 那儿 的
No still have good many places but there

Cháng chéng zuì hǎo kàn.
长 城 最好 看。
Great Wall the best to see

A: It's beautiful. Can we go up on the wall?
Shì hén měi. Wǒ men néng dào Cháng chéng
是 很 美。我们 能 到 长 城
Is very beautiful we can to reach Great Wall

shàng miàn qù kàn kan ma?
上 面 去 看看 吗？
the top to go have a look

B: Certainly. We will buy tickets and go up.
Dāng rán ké yǐ. Mǎi wán piào zài shàng qù.
当 然 可以。买 完 票 再 上 去。
Of course may to buy finish ticket then up to go

A: This is very high! But it's a great feeling to be on the Great Wall. Do you know how long is it?
Zhè li zhēn gāo a! Zhàn zài Cháng chéng shàng
这里 真 高 啊！站 在 长 城 上
Here really high to stand at Great Wall on

gǎn júe zhēn hǎo. Nǐ zhī dào tā yǒu duō cháng ma?
感觉 真 好。你 知道 它 有 多 长 吗?
to feel really good you to know it has how long

B: It is more than 6000km long and mostly on the mountains.
Dà yūe lìu qiān gōng li cháng, zhu yào jiàn zài
大约 六千 公里 长，主要 建 在
About 6 thousand kms long mainly constructed at

shān shàng.
山 上。
mountain on

A: It's really great. That's why it is clearly visible even from the moon.
Dí qùe liǎo bù qǐ. Suó yǐ tā shèn zhì ké yǐ cóng
的确 了不起。所以 它 甚至 可以 从
Indeed terrific therefore it even may from

Yuè qíu shàng kàn dào.
月球 上 看到。
moon above visible

B: Next we are going to see the Ming tombs.
Jiē xià lái wǒ men qù cān guān Míng líng.
接下来 我们 去 参观 明 陵
To continue we to go visit Ming tomb

A: What's this?
Shén me líng?
什 么 陵？
What tomb

B: These are the graves of the Ming dynasty kings, who were buried here.
Jìu shì Míng cháo huáng dì de líng mù.
就 是 明 朝 皇 帝 的 陵 墓。
Just are Ming dynasty king's tomb

A: What next?
Xiàn zài qù nǎ er?
现 在 去 哪 儿
Now to go where

B: Next we are going to Tian-an-men square.
Xiàn zài qù yóu lǎn Tiān-ān-mén guáng chǎng.
现 在 去 游 览 天 安 门 广 场。
Now to go to visit Tian-an-men square

A: Great. This is very famous.
Hǎo ā. Tā fēi cháng yǒu míng.
好 啊。它 非 常 有 名。
Good it extremely famous

B: Yes. This is the biggest square in the world.
Duì. Tā shì shì jiè shàng zuì dà de guáng chǎng.
对。它 是 世界 上 最大 的 广 场。
Right it is the world in the biggest square

A: Really? I have heard this is surrounded by big buildings.
Zhēn dē? Wǒ tīng shuō tā sì zhōu dōu yǒu
真 的？我 听 说 它 四 周 都 有
Really I heard it four side all have

hóng wěi jiàn zhù.
宏 伟 建 筑。
grand building

B: Yes. If you enter from Qianmen side, you will find yourself in the back of Mao's Memorial Hall.
Shì de. Rù guǒ nǐ cóng Qián mén fāng xiàng jìn qù, nǐ
是的。如果 你 从 前门 方 向 进去，你
Yes if you from Qian men direction go in you

shǒu xiān kàn dào de shì Máo zhu xí jì niàn táng de bèi miàn.
首 先 看 到 的 是 毛 主 席 纪 念 堂 的 背 面。
first of all to see is Mao Chairman memorial back side

A: Mao holds a significant place in Chinese history.
Máo zhu xí zài Zhōng guó lì shǐ shàng jǔ zú qīng zhòng.
毛 主 席 在 中 国 历史 上 举 足 轻 重。
Mao Chairman at China history on prove decisive

B: Yes. On it's left side is the Great Hall of the People.
Méi cuò. Jì niàn táng zuǒ biān shì Rén mín dà huì táng.
没 错。纪 念 堂 左 边 是 人 民 大 会 堂。
Not wrong memorial left side is the Great Hall of People

A: Is this the place where Chinese parliament functions?
Xiāng dāng yú Zhōng guó de yì huì dà shà ma?
相 当 于 中 国 的 议会 大 厦 吗?
Correspond to China parliament building

B: You can say like that.
Nǐ ké yǐ zhè me shuō.
你 可以 这 么 说。
You can like this to say

This place is also used for meeting foreign guests, convening of party meetings etc.
Nà li hái yòng lái jiē dài wài bīn, zhāo kāi
那里 还 用 来 接 待 外 宾，召 开
There also be used to receive foreign guests to hold

dǎng de dài biǎo dà huì déng deng.
党 的 代 表 大 会 等 等。
party's representative meeting etc.etc.

On the right side of Mao's memorial is the Museum of Chinese History.
Zài jì niàn táng yòu biān shì Zhōng guó lì shi bó wù guǎn
在 纪 念 堂 右 边 是 中 国 历史 博 物 馆。
At memorial right side is China history museum

A: That will be very interesting.
Nà er yí dìng hén yǒu yì si.
那 儿 一 定 很 有 意思。
There definitely very interesting

B: Yes. There you can have a glance at the history of one of the oldest civilizations on earth.
Dāng rán. Zài nà er nǐ kě yǐ yì dǔ dì qíu
当 然。在 那儿 你 可以 一睹 地球
Of course at there you can to see earth

shàng zuì gú lǎo de wén míng zhī yī.
上 最 古老 的 文 明 之一。
on the most ancient civilizaton one of the

A: Where is the forbidden city?
Zǐ jìn chéng zài nǎ gè fāng xiàng?
紫禁城 在 哪个 方 向?
Forbidden city at which direction

B: It's on the other side of Tian-an-men square.
Jìu zài Tiān-ān-mén guáng chǎng de qián miǎn.
就 在 天 安 门 广 场 的 前 面。
Just at Tian-an-men square front side

A: Is this the place where China's last Emperor lived?
Shì Zhōng guó mò dài huáng dì céng jīng jū zhù de dì fāng?
是 中 国 末 代 皇 帝 曾 经 居住 的 地方?
Is China the last emperor (in past) to live place

B: Yes. That's why it is also known as the Imperial Palace.
Shì de. Suó yǐ shuō tā hái jiào zuò Gù gōng.
是 的。所 以 说 它 还 叫 作 故 宫。
Yes therefore to say it still to be called Old palace

A: Can we go in?

Wǒ mén néng jìn qù ma?

我们 能 进 去 吗？

We can to enter to go

B: Certainly. There is a gate tower at the entrance of the Palace.

Dāng rán kě yǐ. Zài rù kǒu chù shì Tiān-ān-mén chéng lóu

当然可以。在入口处 是 天安门 城楼

Of course can at entrance is Tian-an-men city tower

From there chairman Mao declared the formation of New China.

Cóng nà er Máo zé dōng zhu xí xuān gào xīn

从 那儿 毛泽东 主席 宣告 新

From there Mao Ze Dong chairman to declare new

Zhōng guó chéng lì.

中国 成立。

China establish

In the middle of the square is the Memorial of People's Heroes.

Zài guáng chǎng zhōng yāng shì Rén mín

在 广场 中央 是 人民

At square centre is People's

yīng xióng jì niàn bēi.

英雄 纪念碑。

Heroes Memorial

A: What is this on the side of the Imperial Palace?
Zài gù gōng páng biān shì shén me?
在 故宫 旁边 是 什么？
at old palace on the side is what

B: This is the memorial garden for Dr. Sun Yat-sen.
Shì zhōng shān gōng yuán.
是 中山 公园。
Is Sun yat-sen garden

A: Which are we going to see next?
Jiē xià lái wǒ men qù ná lǐ?
接下来 我们 去 哪里？
To continue we to go where

B: Now we are going to the Summer Palace.
Dào Yí hé yuán wán er qù.
到 颐和园 玩儿 去。
To reach Summer Palace enjoy to go

A: What is that?
Shì shén me dì fāng a?
是 什么 地方 啊？
Is what place

B: It's a imperial park with a lake, a hill and a Imperial Palace inside.
Shì yí gè yǒu shān yóu shuǐ de huáng jiā gōng yuán.
是 一个 有山有水 的 皇家 公园。
Is one have hills have water emperor's family garden

It was the summer home of the king.
Tā céng jīng shì huáng dì de xià gōng.
它 曾经 是 皇 帝 的 夏 宫。
It (in the past) was emperor's summer palace

A: Is the palace still being used?
Xiàn zài hái yǒu rén zhù ma?
现 在 还有 人 住 吗?
At present still have person to stay

B: No. It has been converted into a museum.
Méi yǒu le. Xiàn zài yǐ jīng gǎi wéi bó wù guǎn le.
没 有 了。现 在 已经 改 为 博 物 馆 了。
Not have at present already to change as musuem

A: This place is really beautiful.
Zhè gè dì fāng zhēn shì tài měi le.
这 个 地 方 真 是 太 美 了。
This place really is too beautiful

B: Indeed. In the winters, the lake becomes ice and lot of people come here for ice skating.
Nǐ shuō de méi cuò. Dào le dōng tiān, hú miàn dōu
你 说 的 没 错。到 了 冬 天，湖 面 都
You to say not wrong to reach witner lake surface all

jié le bīng, yǒu hěn duō rén zài bīng shàng huá bīng ne.
结了冰，有 很 多 人 在 冰 上 滑 冰 呢。
to ice up have many people at ice on ice skating

A: Is that all?
Guàng wán le ma?
逛 完了 吗?
Sight seeing finished

B: Yes. This is all for the day.
Jīn tiān guàng wán le.
今天 逛 完 了。
Today sight seeing finished

But there are more places in Beijing, which are worth seeing.
Dàn běi jīng hái yǒu hěn duō zhí de yí kàn dé dì fāng.
但 北京 还有 很多 值得一看 的 地方。
But Beijing still have many worth to see place

We will go to see those places at some other time.
Yǐ hòu yǒu shí jiān wǒ men zài qù.
以后 有 时间 我们 再 去。
Later have time we again to go

A: Definitely. We had a wonderful time today.
Yí dìng děi qù. Jīn tiān wǒ men wán er de
一定 得 去。今天 我们 玩儿 得
Definitely must to go today we to enjoy

zhēn gāo xìng.
真 高 兴。
real happy

Thank you for your company.
Xìe xìe nǐ péi wǒ.
谢谢 你 陪 我。
Thank you to accompany me

B: Not at all. It's pleasure being with you.
Bú yòng kè qì. Gēn nǐ zài yí kuài er wǒ yě hěn gāo xìng.
不用 可气。跟你 在 一块儿 我也 很 高兴。
No need polite with you at together I also very happy

A: Good bye!
Zài jiàn!
再 见!
See again

B: Good bye!
Zài jiàn!
再 见!
See again

Addl. Vocabulary

Tour Guide	*dǎo yóu*	导 游
Monument	*jì niàn bēi*	纪 念 碑

Opera House	*jù yuàn*	剧 院
Beijing Opera	*jīng jù*	京 剧
Concert Hall	*yīn yuè tīng*	音 乐 厅
Acrobatics	*zá jì*	杂 技
Puppet Show	*mù ǒu xì*	木 偶 戏
The Temple of Heaven	*Tiān tán*	天 坛
Beihai Park	*Béi hǎi gōng yuán*	北 海 公 园
The Zoo	*Dòng wù yuán*	动 物 园
The Fragrance Hill	*Xiāng shān*	香 山
Temple of Sleeping Buddha	*Wò fó sì*	卧 佛 寺
Beijing-man Cave	*Běi jīng rén yí zhǐ*	北 京 人 遗 址
Natural History Musuem	*Zì rán lì shǐ bó wù guǎn*	自 然 历 史 博 物 馆
Jingshan Park	*Jǐng shān gōng yuán*	景 山 公 园
Amusement Park	*Yóu lě yuán*	游 乐 园

CHAPTER XVI

In A Restaurant
zài cān guǎn
在 餐 馆

A: It's a holiday today, weather is so good.
Jīn tiān fàng jià, tiān qì yòu hǎo.
今天 放假，天气 又 好。
Today holiday weather also good

Let's eat outside. Can you suggest any good restaurant?
Dào wài miàn chī qù. Nǐ zhī dào nǎ er de
到 外面 吃 去。你 知道 哪儿 的
To outside eat to go you know where

cān guǎn bú cuò ma?
餐 馆 不错 吗？
restaurant good

B: What do you want to eat?
Ní xiǎng chī shén me?
你 想 吃 什么？
You to think eat what

A: I would like to eat Beijing Roasted Duck.
Wǒ xiǎng chī Běi jīng kǎo yā.
我 想 吃 北京 烤鸭。
I to think eat Beijing roasted duck

B: Then let's go to Hepingmen Beijing Duck Restaurant.
Nà jìu dào Hé píng mén kǎo yā diàn ba.
那 就 到 和平门 烤鸭店 吧。
Then just to go Hepingmen roasted duck restaurant

(At the restaurant) (*Zài Fàn diàn*)（在饭店）

A: Welcome, sir! May I help you?
Huān yíng guāng lín! Qǐng wèn xū yào shén me?
欢迎 光临！请问 需要 什么？
Welcome gracious please ask want what

B: Seat for two, please.
Shuāng rén zuò.
双 人 座。
Two persons seat

A: Have you reserved the table, sir?
Qǐng wèn xiān sheng shì fǒu tí qián yù dìng guò?
请问 先生 是否 提前 预订 过？
Please ask Mr./sir whether in advance to reserve

B: No, we haven't.
Méi yǒu.
没 有。
Not have

A: Sorry sir! We are fully booked.
Hěn bào qiàn! Xiān sheng. Wǒ men zhè er yǐ jīng
很 抱 歉！先 生。我 们 这儿 已 经
Very sorry Mr./sir we here already

kè mǎn le.
客 满 了。
full

A: Is there any Fast Food Centre nearby?
Fù jìn yǒu kuài cān diàn mà?
附 近 有 快 餐 店 吗？
Nearby have fast food shop

B: Nearest is Kentucky. Let's go there.
Kěn dé jī zuì jìn. Qù nà er ba.
肯 德鸡 最 近。去 那 儿 吧。
Kentucky the nearest to go there

A: What would you like to eat?
Ní xiǎng chī shén me?
你 想 吃 什 么？
You to think eat what

B: I will take fried chicken, finger chips and coke. What about you?

Wǒ yào zhà jī tuǐ shu tiáo hé kě lè. Nǐ nē?

我 要 炸鸡腿 ，薯 条 和 可乐 你呢？

I want fried chicken leg finger chips and cola you

A: I will go for roasted beef, chicken burger and coffee.

Wǒ xiǎng chī kǎo níu ròu, jī ròu, hàn bǎo bāo hé kā fēi

我 想 吃 烤牛 肉，鸡肉，汉堡包 和 咖啡

I to think eat roasted beef chicken burger and coffee

B: Food was really delicious!

Zhēn shì tài xiāng le!

真 是 太 香 了！

Really is too tasty

A: Now let's have ice-cream. I will take chocolate ice-cream. What about you?

Xiàn zài chī bīng qí lín ba. Wǒ diǎn qiǎo kè lì

现在 吃 冰淇淋吧。我 点 巧克力

Now to eat ice cream I to order chocolate

de. Nǐ yào shén me?

的。你 要 什 么？

you want what

B: I will have strawberry.

Cǎo méi ba.

草 莓 吧。

Strawberry

What sort of food you like, Chinese or western?
Ní xǐ huān chī shén me, zhōng cān hái shì xī cān?
你 喜欢 吃 什 么，中 餐 还是 西餐？
You like to eat what chinese food or western food

Can I take the order sir?
Yào diǎn cài ma? xiān sheng!
要 点 菜 吗？先 生！
Want order food Sir

What do you have in dessert?
Ní zhè li de tián shí dōu yǒu xiē shén me?
你 这里 的 甜 食 都 有 些 什 么？
You here sweet food all have some what

Get me a bottle of beer.
Lái yì píng pí jiǔ.
来 一 瓶 啤 酒。
To bring one bottle beer

Please bring it fast. We are in a hurry.
Qǐng shàng cài kuài diǎn. Wǒ men yǒu jí shì.
请 上 菜 快 点。我 们 有 急事。
Please to bring food fast a bit we have urgent work

Is there any cheaper restaurant here?
Zhè er yǒu gèng shí huì de cān guǎn ma?
这 儿 有 更 实 惠 的 餐 馆 吗？
Here have more cheap restaurant

Have you finished sir?

Nín chī wán le ma, xiān sheng?

您 吃 完 了 吗，先 生？

You to eat finished Mr./sir

May I have the cheque (bill) please?

Qǐng ná zhàng dān lái.

请 拿 帐 单 来。

Please to get bill to bring

The food was good. We enjoyed it.

Zhè li de cāi zuò dé bú cuò. Wǒ men hén xǐ huān.

这里的菜 做 得 不错。我们 很 喜欢。

Here food to prepare not bad we very to like

Addl. Vocabulary

McDonald	*mài dāng láo*	麦 当 劳
Sichuan Restaurant	*chuān cài guǎn*	川 菜 馆
Pizza	*pī sà bǐng*	披 萨 饼
Hamburger	*hàn bǎo bāo*	汉 堡 包
Packed Meal	*hé fàn*	盒 饭

Fried Rice	*chǎo fàn*	炒饭
Fried Noodles	*chǎo miàn*	炒面
Fried Prawns	*zhá duì xiā*	炸对虾
Fish	*yǘ*	鱼
Bean Curd	*dòu fu*	豆腐
Soup	*tāng*	汤
Sea Food	*hǎi xiān*	海鲜
Boiled Egg	*zhu jī dàn*	煮鸡蛋
Milk	*niu nǎi*	牛奶
Milk Powder	*nai fěn*	奶粉
Bread	*miàn bāo*	面包
Cake	*dàn gāo*	蛋糕
Pastry	*diǎn xīn*	点心
Sandwich	*sān míng zhì*	三明治
Curd/Yogurt	*suān nǎi*	酸奶
Sausages	*xiāng cháng*	香肠
Plate	*pán zi*	盘子

Spoon	*sháo zi*	勺 子
Fork	*chā zi*	叉 子
Knife	*dāo zi*	刀 子
Chopsticks	*kuài zi*	筷 子
Glass	*bēi zi*	杯 子
Napkins	*cān jīn zhǐ*	餐 巾 纸
Ashtray	*yān huī gāng*	烟 灰 缸
Toothpick	*yá qiān*	牙 签
Tinned Food	*guàn tóu shí pǐn*	罐 头 食 品
Packed Food	*dài zhuāng shí pǐn*	袋 装 食 品

CHAPTER XVII

Shopping
Gòu wù
购 物

A: I want to go for shopping. Could you suggest a good market?
Wǒ xiǎng qù gòu wù, nǐ néng jiè shào hǎo
我 想 去 购物，你 能 介 绍 好
I think go shopping you can to introduce good

yì diǎn de shāng chǎng ma?
点 的 商 场 吗？
a bit market

B: What do want to buy?
Nǐ xiǎng mǎi shén me?
你 想 买 什 么？
You to think to buy what

A: I want to buy some daily use items.
Wǒ xiǎng mǎi xiē rì yòng pǐn.
我 想 买 些 日 用 品。
I think to buy some daily use items

B: Let's go to Wangfujing Departmental store. You can buy many things from there.
Nà wǒ men dao Wáng fu jǐng bǎi huò dà lóu. Nǐ
那 我 们 到 王 府 井 百 货 大 楼。你
Then we to go Wangfujing departmental store you—

ké yǐ còng nà er mǎi hěn duō dōng xi.
可以 从 那儿 买 很 多 东 西。
may from there to buy many things

A: Are there any other markets here?
Hái yǒu qí tā shì chǎng ma?
还 有 其它 市 场 吗？
Still have other market

B: Yes, there are so many like Xidan, Dongdan, Qianmen etc.
Yǒu hěn duō, bǐ rù Xī dān, Dōng dān, Qián mén děng.
有 很 多，比如 西单，东 单， 前 门 等。
Have many like Xidan Dongdan Qianmen etc

A: Are there any free market here?
Yǒu lián jïà shì chǎng ma?
有 廉 价 市 场 吗？
Have reduce price market

B: Yes, there are wholesale markets for ordinary items such as Tiancheng, Tianwaitian etc..

Yǒu ā. Yì bān jiào xiǎo shāng pǐn pī fā
有啊。一般 叫 小 商 品 批发
Yes normally to call small items wholesale

shì chǎng, rú Tiān chéng, Tiān wài tiān déng děng.
市场，如 天 成，天外天 等 等。
market like Tiancheng Tianwaitian etc.etc.

A: What is the price of that shirt?
Nà jiàn chèn shān duō shao qián?
那件 衬 衫 多少 钱？
That shirt how much money

B: You want half sleeve or full sleeve?
Nǐ yào duǎn xìu hái shì cháng xìu?
你要 短 袖 还是 长 袖？
You want short sleeve or long sleeve

A: I want two half sleeve and one full sleeve.
Wǒ yào liǎng jiàn duǎn xìu, yí jiàn cháng xìu.
我要 两 件 短 袖，一件 长 袖。
I want two short sleeve one long sleeve

B: Which size do you want?
Shén me chǐ cùn de?
什么 尺寸 的？
What size

A: I want larger size.
Dà hào de.
大 号 的。
Large size

Is it cotton, terricot mix or pure cotton?
Shì hún fǎng de hái shì chún mián dē?
是 混 纺 的 还 是 纯 棉 的？
Is terricot or cotton

B: It is 100% pure cotton.
Bǎi fēn zhī bǎi chún mián.
百 分 之 百 纯 棉。
Percent hundred cotton

A: Do you have silk shirts?
Ní yǒu sī chóu chèn shān ma?
你 有 丝 绸 衬 衫 吗？
You have silk shirt

Can I try it on?
Wǒ néng shì shi ma?
我 能 试 试 吗？
I can try

This one is little large, do you have smaller one?
Zhè jiàn yǒu diǎn dà, nǐ yǒu jiàn xiǎo de ma?
这 件 有 点 大，你 有 件 小 的 吗？
This have a bit large you have one small

I also want jeans pant and cotton T-shirts.
Wǒ hái yào níu zǐ kù hé mián T- xu.
我 还 要 牛仔裤 和 棉 T-恤。
I also want jeans pant and cotton T-shirt

Could you show me more in different colours?
Nǐ néng ràng wǒ tiāo yì tiāo yán sè ma?
你 能 让 我 挑一挑 颜色 吗？
You can let me to choose colour

B: We have only this in our stock.
Wǒ men zhí yǒu zhè zhǒng yán sè.
我们 只有 这 种 颜 色。
we only have this type colour

A: I want something to match this.
Wǒ yào néng hé zhè gè dā pèi de.
我 要 能 和 这个 搭配 的。
I want can with this to match

B: Sorry, it's sold out.
Duì bù qǐ, mài wán le.
对不起，卖 完 了。
Sorry to sell finish

A: Is it your last price?
Ké yǐ zài pián yì diǎn ma?
可以 再 便宜 点 吗？
can more cheap a bit

B: All the prices are fixed. No bargaining.
Suó yǒu jià gé dōu shì gù dìng de. Bù néng
所 有 价格 都 是 固 定 的。不 能
All price all are fixed cannot

tǎo jià huán jià.
讨 价 还 价。
to bargain

A: How much I have to pay?
Wǒ děi fù duō shao?
我 得 付 多 少？
I must to pay how much

I also want some socks/hats/handkerchiefs.
Wǒ hái yào mǎi jǐ shuāng wà zi, jí dǐng
我 还 要 买 几 双 袜 子，几顶
I also want to buy some pair socks some

mào zi, jǐ zhāng shǒu juàn.
帽 子，几 张 手 绢。
hat some hankerchief

B: Please go to the counter on the opposite side.
Qǐng dào duì mian de guì tái.
请 到 对 面 的 柜 台。
Please go to opposite side counter

A: Do you have leather shoes/canvas shoes?
Nǐ zhè er yǒu pí xié / bù xié ma?
你 这 儿 有 皮鞋/布 鞋 吗？
You here have leather shoes/canvas shoes

B: Which size you want?
Nǐ yào duō dà hào de?
你 要 多 大 号 的？
You want how big size

A: I want 26/27cm size.
Wǒ yào èr shí lìu / èr shí qī lí mǐ de.
我 要 二十六/二十七 厘米 的。
I want twenty six twenty seven cms

B: With laces or without laces?
Yào xié dài de hái shì méi yǒu xié dài de?
要 鞋 带 的 还 是 没 有 鞋 带 的？
Want shoe laces or without shoe laces

A: I want to see both.
Liáng zhǒng dōu kàn kan.
两 种 都 看 看。
Two type both have a look.

Do you have this in brown/black/white colour?
Ní yǒu zhè zhǒng zōng sè/ hēi sè/ bāi sè de ma?
你 有 这 种 棕 色/ 黑色/ 白 色 的吗？
You have this type brown black white

Have you got any other design?
Nǐ hái yǒu qí tā yàng shì ma?
你 还 有 其它 样 式 吗？
You still have other style

I want in flat/small/high heel.
Wǒ yào píng/ dī / gāo gēn de.
我 要 平 / 低 / 高 跟 的。
You want flat low high heel

Do you have ladies sandals / children shoes?
Nǐ zhè er yǒu nǚ shì liáng xié / tóng xié ma?
你 这儿 有 女式 凉 鞋 / 童 鞋 吗？
You here have lady sandal children shoe

This leather is very hard. I want soft leather.
Zhè xié de pí tài yìng, wǒ yào ruǎn yì diǎn de.
这 鞋 的皮 太 硬，我 要 软 一点 的。
This shoe leather too hard I want soft a bit

How much is it altogether?
Zǒng gòng duō shao qián?
总 共 多 少 钱？
Altogether how much money

B: It is...yuan.
Zǒng gòng.... qián.
总 共.... 钱。
Altogether ....money

A: Where can I get thermosbottle/iron/umbrella/blanket?
Nǎ er néng mǎi dào rè shuǐ píng/ diàn yùn dǒu/ sǎn/ tǎn zi?
哪儿能 买到 热水瓶/电熨斗/伞/毯子?
Where can buy thermos bottle iron press umbrella blanket

B: You please go upstairs.
Qǐng shàng lóu.
请 上 楼。
Please upper floor

A: How much for a *jin* (half kg) of tomato/onion?
Yì jīn (bàn gōng jīn) xī hóng shì/ yáng cōng duō shao qián?
一斤(半公斤)西红柿/洋葱 多少 钱?
One *jin* (Half kg.) tomato onion how much money

B: Tomato is 2.5yuan per *jin* and onion is 3 yuan per *jin*.
Xī hóng shì èr kuài wǔ yì jīn, yáng cōng sān kuài yì jīn.
西红柿 二块五 一斤,洋葱 三 块 一斤。
Tomato 2 yuan 5 one *jin* onion 3 yuan one *jin*

A: Your rates are very high.
Nǐ de jià tài gāo le.
你的 价 太 高 了。
Your rate very high

B: How much you give?
Nǐ gěi duō shao?
你 给 多 少？
You give how much

A: I will give you 1.5 yuan for tomato and 2 yuan for onion.
Wǒ géi nǐ xī hóng shì yí kuài wǔ yì jīn,
我 给 你 西 红 柿 一 块 五 一 斤，
I to give you tomato 1 yuan 5 one *jin*

yáng cōng liǎng kuài yì jīn.
洋 葱 两 块 一 斤。
onion 2 yuan one *jin*

B: OK! How much you want?
Xíng! Yào duō shao?
行！要 多 少？
OK want how much

A: I want 3 *jin* each.
Měi yàng dōu yào sān jīn.
每 样 都 要 三 斤。
Each kind both want 3 *jin*

How much is for banana/apples?
Xiāng jiāo / píng guǒ duō shao qián yì jīn?
香 蕉 / 苹 果 多 少 钱 一 斤？
Banana apple how much money one *jin*

B: Both 6 yuan one *jin.*
Liǎng yàng dōu shì lìu kuài qián yǐ jīn.
两样 都 是 六块 钱 一斤。
Two types both are 6 yuan money one *jin*

A: Give me 2 *jin* banana and 4 *jin* apple.
Gěi wǒ lái liǎng jīn xiāng jiāo sì jīn píng guǒ.
给我来 两斤 香蕉 四斤 苹果。
Give me 2 *jin* banana 4 *jin* apple

B: Anything else?
Hái yào shén me?
还 要 什么？
Still want what

A: No, that's all. How much I have to pay?
Gòu le. Yí gòng yào duō shao qián?
够了。一共 要 多少 钱？
Enough altogether want how much money

B: Altogether 46.5 yuan.
Quán bù jiā qǐ lái sì shí lìu kuài wǔ.
全部 加起来 四十六块 五。
All put together forty six yuan five

Addl. Vocabulary

Super Market	*chāo jí shì chǎng*	超 级 市 场
Medical Store	*yào diàn*	药 店
Antique Store	*gú dǒng shāng diàn*	古 董 商 店
Book Store	*shū diàn*	书 店
Stationery Store	*wén jù diàn*	文 具 店
Optician's	*yǎn jìng diàn*	眼 镜 店
Jewellery Shop	*zhū bǎo diàn*	珠 宝 店
Watch Store	*zhōng biǎo diàn*	钟 表 店
Photo Studio	*zhào xiàng guǎn*	照 相 馆
Audio & Video Centre	*yīn xiàng zhì pǐn zhōng xīn*	音 响 制 品 中 心
Handicraft Store	*shǒu gōng yì pǐn shāng diàn*	手 工 艺 品 商 店
Arts and crafts shop	*gōng yì měi shù shāng diàn*	工 艺 美 术 商 店

CHAPTER XVIII

At the Conference
Chū xí huì yì
出席 会议

Mr. Chairman,...........
Zhǔ xí xiān sheng,..........
主席 先生，.........
Chairman Mr. ....

His excellency Mr. ....., the prime minister / president of India / China.
Zūn jìng de.... xiān sheng, Zhōng guó / Yìn dù
尊敬 的... 先 生，中 国 / 印 度
Respected .... Mr. China India

zǒng tǒng / zǒng lǐ gé xià.
总 统 / 总 理 阁 下。
President P.M. His Excellency

Members of the presidium.
Zài zhǔ xí tái jìu zuò de dài biǎo men.
在 主席台 就 坐 的 代 表 们。
At presidium just seated delegates

Ladies and gentlemen.
Nǚ shì men, xiān sheng men.
女 士 们， 先 生 们。
Ladies gentlemen

I declare the meeting open.
Wǒ xūan bù huì yì kāi shǐ.
我 宣 佈 会 议 开 始。
I to declare meeting to start

The meeting will be held for three days.
Huì yì jiāng jǔ xíng sān tiān.
会 议 将 举 行 三 天。
Meeting will to hold three days

Today's meeting will be held in three sessions.
Jīn tiān de huì yì yǒu sān gè bù fèn.
今 天 的 会 议 由 三 个 部 分。
Today meeting have three session / part

The first/second/third session will be chaired by.....
Dì yī / dì èr / dì sān gè bù fèn yóu.... zhǔ chí.
第一 / 第二 / 第三 个 部 分 有… 主 持。
First second third session by ...... to chair

The agenda is as follows:
Huì yì yì chéng rú xià:
会 议 议 程 如 下：
Meeting agenda follows

Today the focus of our discussion will on.............
Jīn tiān wǒ men tǎo lùn de zhòng diǎn shì......
今天 我们 讨论 的 重点 是....
Today our to discuss focal point is..........

Are there any suggestions for additions/amendments in the proposed agenda?
Duì yì chéng yǒu méi yǒu bǔ chōng hé xīu zhèng?
对 议程 有没有 补充 和 修正？
For agenda have or not additions and amendments

There will be five speakers.
Jīn tiān yǒu wǔ wèi fā yán rén.
今天 有 五位 发言人。
Today have five speakers

The first point on agenda is......
Yì chéng de dì yī xiàng shì........
议程 的 第一项 是.....
Agenda the first item is..........

The first speaker will be Mr./Mrs. ..... from........
Dì yī wèi fā yán rén shì lái zì... de..... xiān sheng/ nǔ shǐ.
第一位 发言人 是 来自..的..先生 / 女士。
First speaker is come from....... Mr. Mrs.

Please allow me to speak on behalf of the Indian/ Chinese delegation.
Qǐng yǔn xǔ wǒ dài biǎo Yìn dù/ Zhōng guó dài biǎo tuán fā yán.
请 允 许 我 代 表 印 度/ 中 国 代 表 团 发 言。
Please allow me to represent India China delegation to speak

We are in agree/diagree with........ delegate's view.
Wǒ men tóng yì/bù tóng yì... dài biǎo de guān diǎn.
我 们 同 意/不 同 意 . . . 代 表 的 观 点。
We agree disagree ... delegate's viewpoint

Shall we put the motion to a vote?
Wǒ men shì fǒu yīng gāi jìu cǐ dòng yì jìn xíng biǎo júe?
我 们 是 否 应 该 就 此 动 议 进 行 表 决?
We whether or not should just this motion to carry out vote

The motion is passed unanimously/by majority vote.
Cǐ xiàng dòng yì huò yí zhì tōng guò/ duō shù tōng guò.
此 项 动 议 获 一 致 通 过/ 多 数 通 过。
This motion to achieve unanimous through majority through

We protest/ strongly protest such remarks.
Wǒ men duì cǐ biǎo shì fǎn duì/ qiáng lie fǎn duì.
我 们 对 此 表 示 反 对/ 强 烈 反 对。
We towards it to express protest strong protest

The session is adjourned for the lunch/ coffee break.
Huì yì xīu huì, xiàn zài shì wǔ cān/zhōng jiān xīu xi shí jiān.
会 议 休 会, 现 在 是 午 餐/ 中 间 休 息 时 间。
Meeting adjourn now is lunch middle rest time

The session is adjourned for the day.
Huì yì xīu huì yì tiān.
会议 休会 一天。
Meeting adjourn one day

I declare the meeting closed.
Wǒ xuān bù, huì yì jíe shù.
我 宣佈，会议 结束。
I to declare meeting to conclude

The meeting has drawn successful conclusion
Huì yì qǔ dé yuán mǎn chéng gōng.
会议 取得 圆满 成功。
Meeting to achieve satisfactory success

We had a very fruitful exchange of views.
Wǒ men jìn xíng le fù yǒu chéng xiào de jiāo líu.
我们 进行 了富有 成效 的 交流。
We carried out very fruitful exchange of views.

We learnt a lot from each others experiences.
Wǒ men hù xiāng jí qǔ le bǎo guì de jīng yàn.
我们 互相 汲取 了 宝贵 的 经验。
We mutual to draw valuable experience

Addl. Vocabulary

Symposium	*yán tǎo huì*	研讨会
Workshop	*zhuān tí tǎo lùn huì*	专题讨论会
Head of the delegation	*Tuán zhǎng*	团长
Observer	*guān chá yuán*	观察员
Round table conference	*yuán zhūo huì yì*	圆桌会议
Group discussion	*fēn zǔ tǎo lùn*	分组讨论
Joint work group	*lián hé gōng zuò zǔ*	联合工作组
Joint declaration	*lián hé shēng míng*	联合声明
Agreement	*xié yì*	协议
Press briefing	*xīn wén fā bù huì*	新闻发佈会
Press conference	*xīn wén zhāo dài huì*	新闻招待会
Mutual co-opertion	*xiāng hù hé zuò*	相互合作
Mutual understanding	*hù xiāng lǐ jǐe*	互相理解

Five Principles of Peaceful Co-existence
Hé píng gòng chǔ wǔ xiàng yuán zé
和平 共处 五项 原则

CHAPTER XIX

Business Chinese
Shāng mào Hàn yǔ
商 贸 汉 语

Inquiry
Xún jià
询 价

I am from... company. This is my card.
Wǒ shì... gōng sī de. Zhè shì wǒ de míng piàn.
我 是... 公 司的。这 是 我 的 名 片。
I am..... company this is my name card

What can I do for you?
Yǒu hé guì gàn?
有 何 贵 干？
What can I do for you

We are interested in starting import/export business with China.
Wǒ men duì yǔ Zhōng guó zuò jìn-chū kǒu shēng yì
我 们 对 与 中 国 做 进 出 口 生 意
We towards with China to do import export business

hén gǎn xìng qù.
很 感 兴 趣。
very to be interested

May I know what kind of items are you interested in?
Ní néng gào sù wǒ nǐ men duì shén me xiàng mù
你 能 告诉 我 你们 对 什么 项 目
You can to tell me you for what item

gǎn xìng qù ma?
感 兴 趣 吗？
interest

We are particularly interested in hardware/arts and crafts.
Wǒ men duì yìng jiàn/gōng yì pǐn tè bié gǎn xìng qù.
我们 对 硬 件/工 艺 品 特别 感 兴 趣。
We for hardware art&craft item especially interest

Do you have detailed catalogue of these products?
Ní yǒu zhè xiē chán pǐn de xiǎng xì mù lù ma?
你 有 这些 产 品 的 详 细 目 录 吗？
You have these product detail catalogue

This is our inquiry. Would you like to have a look at it?
Zhè jiù shì wǒ men de xún jià dān. Qǐng nín guò mù.
这 就 是 我 们 的 询 价 单。请 您 过 目。
This just is our inquiry list please you to go through

What is Article Number of this item?
Qíng bǎ zhè gè chán pǐn de pǐn hào gào sù wǒ.
请 把 这个 产 品 的 品 号 告 诉 我。
Please let this product item number to tell me

We hope to do substantial business with your company.
Wǒ men xī wàng néng yǔ guì gōng sī dà liàng chéng jiāo.
我 们 希 望 能 与 贵 公 司 大 量 成 交。
We to hope can with your company large scale business

What type do you want to order?
Ní dǎ suàn dìng gòu ná zhǒng xíng hào de?
你 打 算 定 购 哪 种 型 号 的？
You to plan to purchase which type

Have you got the products of these specifications?
Nǐ men yǒu zhè zhǒng guī gé de chán pǐn ma?
你 们 有 这 种 规 格 的 产 品 吗？
You have this specification product

We are thinking of placing order for this item.
Wǒ men kǎo lǜ dìng gòu zhè zhǒng chán pǐn.
我 们 考 虑 订 购 这 种 产 品。
We plan to to purchase this product

Please let us know about the price.
Qíng nǐ men bào jià.
请 你 们 报 价。
Please you quote price

Offer

Bào jìa

报 价

This is the latest price list. Our prices are very competitve.
Zhè shì wǒ fāng zuì xīn jià mù biǎo. Wǒ fāng
这 是 我 方 最 新 价 目 表。我 方
This is our side the latest price list our side

jià gé hén yǒu jìng zhēng lì.
价 格 很 有 竞 争 力。
price very competitve

Can you give me the better price of this item?
Jià gé néng fǒu zài hé lǐ yì xiē?
价 格 能 否 再 合 理 一 些？
Price whether or not more better some

Could you tell me about your requirement?
Nǐ néng gào sù wǒ guì fāng yào dìng duō shao ma?
你 能 告 诉 我 贵 方 要 订 多 少 吗？
You can to tell us your side want to order how much

We would like to know the price first.
Wǒ men yuàn yì xiān zhī dào jià gé.
我 们 愿 意 先 知 道 价 格。
We wish to first to know price

Until and unless we know the quantity you require, we can not work out the offer.
Wǒ fāng zhí yǒu zài zhī dào guì fāng de xū qíu liàng
我方 只有 在 知道 贵方 的 需求量
Our side only have at to know your side require quantity

yǐ hòu, cái néng bào jià.
以后，才 能 报价。
after only can to quote price

Our requirement is approximately... ton/ ...pieces in a year.
Wǒ men měi nián dà yuē xū yào.. dūn/ ... jiàn.
我们 每年 大约 需要...吨/...件。
We every year about require.... ton .... piece

It will cost you..... US$ per ton/piece.
Nà me mèi dūn/ jiàn de jià gé shì....... měi jīn.
那么 每 吨/件 的 价格 是... 美金。
Then each ton piece price is .... US$

Is it your lowest quotation?
Zhè shì fǒu shì nǐ men de zuì dī jià?
这 是否 是 你们 的 最低价？
This whether is yours the lowest price

Is it C.I.F rate?
Zhè shì dào àn jià ma?
这 是 到岸价 吗？
This is C.I.F. price

No, this is our F.O.B. rate, subject to final confirmation.
Bù, zhè zhǐ shì wǒ fāng de lí àn jià, yǐ wǒ fāng
不，这 只 是 我 方 的 离岸价，以 我 方
No this only is our side F.O.B. rate as well our side

zuì hòu què rèn wéi zhun.
最后 确 认 为 准。
last to decide as accurate

We want C.I.F. New Delhi rate.
Wǒ men xū yào zài Mèng mǎi de dào àn jià.
我们 需要 在 孟 卖 的 到岸价。
We require at Bombay F.O.B. rate

How long does your offer remain valid?
Nǐ men bào jià de yǒu xiào qī shì duō jiǔ?
你们 报价 的 有效期 是 多久？
Your quotation term of validity is how long

It's open for five days.
Wǔ tiān.
五 天。
Five days

Your price is still on the higher side.
Nǐ men de bào jià réng rán hěn gāo.
你们 的 报价 仍然 很 高。
Your quotation still very high

It will be difficult for us to push through the sales at this price.

Wǒ men hěn nán yǐ zhè gè jià gé chéng jiāo.

我们 很 难以 这个 价格 成交。

We very difficult this price to do business

We may reconsider the price if your order is big enough.

Rù guǒ guì fāng yǒu zú gòu de dìng huò, wǒ fāng

如果 贵方 有 足够 的 订货，我方

If your side have enough order goods our side

huì chóng xīn kǎo lǜ jià gé de.

会 重新 考虑 价格 的。

can once again to consider rate

Your quotation is higher than those we got from elsewhere.

Nǐ men de bào jià bǐ qí tā gōng sī yào gāo.

你们 的 报价 比 其它 公司 要 高。

Your quotation than other company have high

Our prices and product quality is better then any other in the international market.

Wǒ fāng bào jià zhī dī hé chán pǐn zhì liàng zhī

我方 报价 之 低 和 产品 质量 之

Our side quotation low and product quality

gāo shì guó jì shì chǎng shàng bù néng bǐ de.

高 是 国际 市场 上 不能 比 的。

high is international market on cannot to compare

If your order is big enough then we can make 2% reduction in our prices.

Rù guǒ guì fāng dìng huò zú gòu duō, nà wǒ fāng

如果 贵方 订货 足够 多，那 我方

If your side order goods sufficient more than our side

huì jiāng bào jià zài tiáo dī bǎi fēn zhī èr.

会 将 报价 再 调 低 百分之二。

can shall quotation again to adjust low percent two

2% is too low. If you give us 5% reduction, then we can go ahead with our order.

Bǎi fēn zhī èr tài shǎo. Rù guǒ nǐ men néng jiàng

百分之二 太 少。如果 你们 能 将

Percent two too less if you can to reduce

bǎi fēn zhī wǔ, wǒ men jìu fā dìng dān.

百分之五，我们 就 发 订单。

percent five we just to give order

We can't reduce it to the price you are indicating.

Wǒ fāng wú fǎ àn guì fāng yāo qíu jiàng jià zhè me duō.

我方 无法 按 贵方 要求 降价 这么 多。

Our side no way as per you side demand to reduce price this much

Since it is our first deal, so we can only give you maximum of 3% reduction.

Dàn jì rán zhè shì wǒ men zhī jiān de dì yī bǐ shēng yì,

但 既然 这是 我们 之间 的 第一笔 生意，

But since this is our between the first deal

wǒ fāng zhǐ néng zhì duō jiàng jià bǎi fēn zhī sān.
我方 只能 至多 将价 百分之三。
our side only can maximum to reduce price percent three

All right. We agree to conclude the transaction at this rate.
Ké yǐ. Wǒ men tóng yì àn cǐ bào jià zuò zhè bǐ
可以。我们 同意 按此 报价 做 这笔
All right we to agree as per this quotation to do this

shēng yì.
生 意。
business

Placing of order
Dìng huò
订 货

What is the minimum quantity of an order for your goods?
Guì fāng zhè zhǒng chán pǐn de qǐ dìng liàng shì
贵方 这种 产品 的 起订量 是
Your side this type product quantity of order is

duō shao?
多 少？
how much

It is 500 ton/ 200 pieces.
Wǔ bǎi dūn / èr bǎi jiàn.
五百 吨 / 二百 件。
Five hundred tons two hundred pieces

All right. We would like to place order for 1500 ton/ 6000 pieces.
Xǐng. Wǒ men dǎ suàn dìng gòu yì qiān wǔ bǎi
行。我们 打算 订购 一千五百
All right we plan to purchase order 1500

dūn/ lìu qiān jiàn.
吨 / 六千 件。
ton 6000 pieces

Can you meet our requirement?
Guì fāng néng mǎn zú wǒ fāng yāo qíu de shù liàng ma?
贵方 能 满足 我方 要求 的 数量 吗？
Your side can to satisfy our side requirement quantity

At present we can supply you 1000 ton/ 4000 pieces.
Xiàn zài wǒ fāng ké yǐ tí gòng yì qiān dūn/ sì qiān
现在 我方 可以 提供 一千 吨 / 四千
At present our side can to supply thousand tons 4000

jiàn gěi guì fāng.
件 给 贵方。
pieces to give your side

We hope to supply the remaining quantity of goods after two months.

Wǒ men jiāng zài yǐ hòu de liǎng gè yuè zhōng

我 们 将 在 以 后 的 两 个 月 中

we shall at later two months in

bu zú shèng xià de bù fèn.

补 足 剩 下 的 部 分。

to make up left over portion

Terms of payment

Fù kuǎn fāng shì

付 款 方 式

We would like to adopt terms of payment by installments for this transaction.

Wǒ men zhè cì jiāo yì jiāng cǎi yòng fēn qī fù kuǎn

我 们 这 次 交 易 将 采 用 分 期 付 款

We this deal shall to adopt installment

fāng shì.

方 式。

method

It is very difficult to accept your suggestion.
Wǒ fāng hěn nān jiē shòu guì fāng jiàn yì.
我 方 很 难 接 受 贵 方 建 议。
Our side very difficult to acept your side suggestion

What is your normal practice about terms of payment?
Yì bān qǐng kuàng xià, guì fāng cǎi yòng shén me
一 般 情 况 下，贵 方 采 用 什 么
In general situation under your side to adopt what

fù kuǎn fāng shì?
付 款 方 式？
payment method

We usually accept payment by irrevocable L/C against shipping documents.
Wǒ men cǎi yòng bù kě chè xiāo de xìn yòng zhèng,
我 们 采 用 不 可 撤 消 的 信 用 证，
We to adopt cannot revoke Letter of Credit

píng zhuāng yùn dān jù jié huì fù kuǎn fāng shì.
凭 装 运 单 据 结 汇 付 款 方 式。
base on shipping papers as guarantee payment method

How about fifty percent by L/C & fifty percent by installments?
Rù guǒ bǎi fēn zhī wǔ shí cǎi yòng xìn yòng zhèng,
如 果 百 分 之 五 十 采 用 信 用 证，
If percent fifty to adopt L/C

bǎi fēn zhī wǔ shí cǎi yòng fēn qī fù kuǎn, guì fāng
百分之 五十 采用 分期付款，贵方
percent fifty to adopt installment your side

rèn wéi rù hé?
认为 如何？
consider how

OK. Your L/C must reach us thirty days before the delivery.
Kéyǐ. Guì fāng de xìn yòng zhèng bì xū zài jiāo huò
可以。贵方 的 信用 证 必须在交货
All right your side L/C must at delivery

qián sān shí tiān nèi fā dào wǒ chù.
前 三十天 内 发到 我 处。
before thirty days inside dispatch to my office

We will open the L/C as soon as we reach back home.
Wǒ men yī huí qù jiu zhuó shǒu bàn lǐ kāi zhèng
我们 一 回去 就 着 手 办理 开 证
We as to return soon as start with to fulfil open L/C

shǒu xù.
手 续。
procedures

Please indicate that your L/C is negotiable in our country.
Qǐng zhù míng xìn yòng zhèng yì fù dì diǎn zài
请 注 明 信 用 证 议付 地点 在
Please to indicate L/C negotiable place at

wǒ guó yǒu xiào.
我 国 有 效。
our country effective

We will also send you the time draft for your acceptance in a few days.
Wǒ fāng yě huì zài zuì jìn jiāng qī piào fā wǎng
我 方 也会 在 最 近 将 期 票 发 往
Our side also can at recent shall draft dispatch to

guì fāng, qǐng guì fāng chéng duì.
贵 方，请 贵 方 承 兑。
your side please your side accept

You must also produce a letter of guarantee by your bank.
Guì fāng bì xū tí gòng yóu guì fāng de yín háng
贵 方 必须 题 供 由 贵 方 的 银 行
Your side must to provide by your side bank

chū jù de bǎo zhèng hán.
出具 的 保 证 函。
to issue guarantee letter

We have already made arrangements for the same with our bankers.
Wǒ fāng yǐ jīng hé wǒ fāng de yín háng ān pái le
我 方 已 经 和 我 方 的 银 行 安 排 了
Our side already with our side bank to arrange

bǎo zhèng hán.
保 证 函。
guarantee letter

Shipment
Zhuāng yùn
装 运

How long will it take to affect the delivery?
Fā huò xū yào duō cháng shí jiān?
发 货 需 要 多 长 时 间？
Delivery require how long time

We make deliveries within three months after the receipt of covering L/C.
Wǒ men zài shōu dào xìn yòng zhèng sān ge yuè nèi
我 们 在 收 到 信 用 证 三 个 月 内
We at to receive L/C three months within

fā huò.
发 货。
delivery

What about special deliveries?
Tè bié fā huò yòu yào duō cháng shí jiān?
特别 发货 又 要 多 长 时 间？
Special delivery more want how long time

It takes longer time, but not more than six months.
Shí jiān shāo cháng yì xiē, dàn bú huì chāo guò lìu gè yuè.
时 间 稍 长 一些，但 不会 超 过 六个月。
Time a bit long some but cannot exceed six months

Can you effect the shipment more promptly?
Nǐ men néng bù néng tí qián yí diǎn jiāo huò?
你们 能不能 提前 一点 交 货？
You whether or not in advance a bit deliver goods

It can be effected within two to three weeks after receipt of your L/C.
Wǒ fāng ké yǐ zài shōu dào guì fāng xìn yòng zhèng
我 方 可以 在 收 到 贵 方 信 用 证
Our side can at to receive your side L/C

hòu de liǎng dào sān zhōu nèi jiāo huò.
后 的 两 到 三 周 内 交 货。
after two to three weeks within deliver goods

How do you ship the goods?
Nǐ men rù hé zhuāng yùn?
你 们 如何 装 运？
You how shipment

We usually do the shipment through regular liners.
Wǒ men tōng cháng cǎi yòng dìng qī chuán yùn fāng shì.
我们 通常 采用 定期 船 运 方式
We often to use regular liner method

When is the earliest you can make the shipment?
Guì fāng zuì zǎo néng zài hé shí fā huò?
贵方 最早 能 在 何时 发货？
Your side the earliest can at what time deliver goods

It will not be earlier than September.
Jǐu yuè fèn yǐ hòu.
九月份 以后。
September after

Will you do the shipment from Hong Kong?
Nǐ men shì fǒu cóng Xiāng gǎng zhuāng chuán?
你们 是否 从 香港 装船？
You whether from Hong Kong shipment

No, it will be done from Shanghai.
Bù, cóng Shàng hǎi.
不，从 上海。
No from Shanghai

Do you allow any quantity difference at the time of loading?

Zhuāng chuán shù liàng shàng nǐ men shì fǒu yún xǔ

装 船 数 量 上 你 们 是 否 允 许

Shipping quantity on you whether to allow

yǒu jī dòng fú dù?

有 机 动 幅 度？

have in reserve margin

Yes. We allow maximum up to 5% if the quantity stipulated, which is according to the contracted price.

Yún xǔ, dàn bù néng chāo guò yuē dìng shù liàng de

允 许，但 不 能 超 过 约 定 数 量 的

To allow but cannot to surpass stipulated quantity

bǎi fēn zhī wǔ, zhè gè chā é yóu hé tóng jià gé jié suàn.

百 分 之 五，这 个 差 额 由 合 同 价 格 结 算。

percent five this difference by contract price to calculate

You will be responsible for the custom duties and service charges on exporting goods.

Guì fāng jiāng fù zé chéng dān guān shuì fèi yòng

贵 方 将 负 责 承 担 关 税 费 用

Your side shall responsible to bear custom duty expenses

hé bàn lǐ chū kǒu de shǒu xù fèi.

和 办 理 出 口 的 手 续 费。

and to handle export formalities expenses

All right. But it will be your responsibility to charter a ship and booking of shipping space.
Méi wèn tí. Dàn nǐ men yīng gāi fù zé zū dìng
没 问 题。但 你 们 应 该 负 责 租 订
No problem but you should to handle to book

chuán zhī cāng wèi.
船 只 舱 位。
ship ship space

How about the packing?
Bāo zhuāng zěn me bàn?
包 装 怎 么 办？
Packing how to handle

We will give you in a very attractive packing. But if you want any changes in that, we will do that.
Wǒ fāng huì tí gòng yōu zhì bāo zhuāng. Rū guǒ
我 方 会 提 供 优 质 包 装。如 果
Our side can to provide top quality packing if

guì fāng yǒu xīn chuàng yì, wǒ fāng dìng néng zuò dào.
贵 方 有 新 创 意，我 方 定 能 做 到。
your side have new idea our side definitely to do

What about the outer packing?
Wài bāo zhuāng yòu rù hé?
外 包 装 又 如 何？
Outer packing also how

We use 25kg cartons which are compatible to international standard.

Wǒ fāng cǎi yòng guó jì biāo zhun de èr shí wǔ

我 方 采 用 国 际 标 准 的 二十五

Our side to use international standard twenty five

gōng jīn zhuāng zhí bǎn xiāng.

公 斤 装 纸 板 箱。

kgs to load carton

Will you give the insurance coverage on goods?

Nǐ men shì fǒu tí gòng huò wù báo xiǎn?

你们 是否 提供 货 物 保 险？

You whether or not provide goods insurance

Yes, we will provide W.P.A. for 110% of the invoiced value.

Shì de. Wǒ men jiāng àn fā piào zǒng jīn é tí gòng

是的。我们 将 按 发票 总金额 提供

Yes we shall as per invoice total value to provide

bǎi fēn zhī yī bǎi yī shí de tóu bǎo shuǐ zì xiǎn.

百 分 之 一百一十 的 投 保 水 渍 险。

percentage one hundred ten With Particular Average(WPA)

Does it include the Risk of Breakage?

Tā shì fǒu bāo hán pò suì xiǎn?

它 是否 包 含 破 碎 险？

It whether or not include risk of breakage

No. If you want to add this, you will have to pay the premium.
Bù bāo hán. Rú guǒ guì fāng yào jiā , nà me zhè bǐ
不 包 含。如果 贵 方 要 加，那么 这笔
Not include if our side want to add then this

báo xiǎn fèi yóu guì fāng chéng dān.
保 险 费 由 贵 方 承 担。
insurance premium by your side to bear

Signing a Contract
Qiān hé tong
签 合 同

When can we have the contract?
Wǒ men shén me shí hòu qiān hé tóng?
我 们 什 么 时 候 签 合 同？
We what time to sign agreement

Here it is. Please check the clauses carefully.
Zhè jìu shì hé tóng. Qǐng zǐ xì chá duì.
这 就 是 合 同。请 仔 细 查 对。
This just is agreement please carefully to check

Don't you think we add a sentence here?
Nǐ men rèn wéi zài cǐ chù jiā yì háng rù hé?
你们 认为 在 此处 加 一行 如何？
You consider at this section to add a line how

Have any other suggestion to make?
Hái yǒu qí tā jiàn yì ma?
还有 其它 建议 吗？
Still have other suggestion

No. It contains basically all we have agreed upon during our negotiations.
Méi yǒu. Tā jī běn hán gài le wǒ men de tán pàn
没有。它基本 涵盖 了 我们 的 谈判
Not have it basically containing we discussion

nèi róng.
内容。
contents

When will it be ready for signatures?
Shén me shí hòu qiān zì shēng xiào?
什么 时后 签字 生效？
What time to sign become effective

Would you like to sign the contract now?
Guì fāng néng fǒu xiàn zài jìu qiān zì?
贵方 能否 现在 就 签字？
Your side whether or not now just to sign

Certainly.
Dāng rán kě yǐ.
当然 可以。
Of course yes.

Please sign your name here.
Qǐng zài cǐ chù qiān zì.
请 在 此处 签字。
Please at this section to sign

This is your copy.
Zhè shì guì fāng bǎo cún de fù běn.
这 是 贵方 保存 的 副本。
This is your side to keep copy

Let us congratulate ourselves on successful conclusion of this transaction between us.
Ràng wǒ men qìng hè zhè bǐ jiāo yì yuán mǎn dá chéng.
让 我们 庆贺 这笔 交易 圆满 达成。
Let us congratulate this deal satisfactory to conclude

Claims
Suǒ péi
索　赔

There is a difference of 25 ton between the actual landing weight and the invoiced weight of consignment.

Dào àn hòu de shí jì zhòng liàng yǔ fā piào

到 岸 后 的 实际 重 量 与 发票

Arrive port after actual weight with invoice

xiāng chā èr shí wǔ dūn.

相 差 二十五 吨。

difference twenty five tons

We are ready to meet your claim for the 20 ton shortweight.

Wǒ fāng jiāng zhun bèi bǔ cháng guì fāng tí chū

我方 将 准备 补偿 贵方 提出

Our side shall to prepare to compensate your side to raise

de èr shí dūn quē é.

的 二十 吨 缺额。

twenty tons difference

The goods were not up to the international inspection standard.

Zhè pī huò wù méi yǒu dá dào guó jì jiǎn cè

这 批 货 物 没 有 达 到 国 际 检 测

These goods not have attain international inspection

biāo zhun.

标 准。

standard

We are lodging claim for inferior quality.

Duì qí zhì liàng bù hé gé, wǒ men yāo qíu suǒ péi.

对 其 质 量 不 合 格，我 们 要 求 索 赔。

For its quality not upto the mark we demand to claim

We cannot entertain your claim.

Wǒ fāng bù néng shòu lǐ guì fāng suǒ péi.

我 方 不 能 受 理 贵 方 索 赔。

Our side cannot to accept your side claim

The goods were inspected by the inspection bureau, which is compatible to international standards.

Zhè pī huò wù jīng yóu zhì jiǎn jú jiǎn cè,

这 批 货 物 经 由 质 检 局 检 测，

These goods through by inspection bureau to inspect

wán quán fu hé guó jì biāo zhun.

完 全 符 合 国 际 标 准。

completely compatible international standard

What about the damaged goods?
Pò sun de huò wù zěn me bàn?
破损 的 货物 怎么 办？
Damaged goods how to handle

We wonder if the damage was caused during the transit.
Wǒ men bù néng què dìng pò sun shì fǒu shì zài
我们 不能 确定 破损 是否 是 在
We cannot determine damage whether is at

yùn shū tú zhōng zào chéng de.
运输 途中 造成 的。
transport on the way be a result of

It did not occur during transit. It was due to the rough handling during the loading at the dock.
Bù shì yóu yǘ yùn shū, ér shì yóu yú zhuāng chuán
不是由于运输，而是由于 装 船
Not is because transportation but is because load a ship

shí yě mán zhuāng yùn zào chéng de pò sun.
时 野蛮 装运 造成 的 破损。
that time rough shipment resulting in to damage

You should refer your claim to insurance company for any damage happened during the transit.

Nǐ men yīng gāi jiāng yīn yùn shū zào chéng de

你们 应 该 将 因 运 输 造 成 的

You should let due to transportation created

pò sun xiàng báo xiǎn gōng sī tí chū suǒ péi yāo qíu.

破损 向 保 险 公 司 提 出 索 赔 要 求。

damage to insurance company to raise claim demand

Addl. Vocabulary

Joint Venture	*hé zī qǐ yè*	**合资企业**
Company	*gōng sι*	**公司**
Limited Company	*yǒu xiàn gōng sī*	**有限公司**
Private enterprise	*mín yíng qǐ yè*	**民营企业**
Public Sector	*guó yíng qǐ yè*	**国营企业**
Factory	*gōng chǎng*	**工厂**
Showroom	*huò pǐn chén liè shì*	**货品陈列室**

Assign	*fēn pèi*	分配
Managing Director	*dǒng shì zhǎng*	董事长
Director	*dǒng shì*	董事
Board of Directors	*dǒng shì huì*	董事会
General Manager	*zǒng jīng lǐ*	总经理
Manager	*jīng lǐ*	经理
Coorperate	*hé zuò*	合作
Trade Fair	*jiāo yì huì*	交易会
Invitation Letter	*yāo qǐng xìn*	邀请信
Two Sides	*shuāng fāng*	双方
Light Industry	*qīng gōng yè*	轻工业
Heavy Industry	*zhòng gōng yè*	重工业
Interest Rate	*lì xī*	利息
Equipment	*shè bèi*	设备
Technology Transfer	*jì shù zhuǎn ràng*	技术转让
Market	*shì chǎng*	市场
Market Price	*shì chǎng jià*	市场价

Customer	*gù kè*	顾客
Spare Parts	*líng pèi jiàn*	零配件
Assemble	*zǔ zhuāng*	组装
Raw Material	*yuán liào*	原料
Brand	*pǐn pái*	品牌
Order Form	*dìng dān*	订单
Discount	*yōu huì*	优惠
Commission	*wěi yuán huì*	委员会
Capital	*zī chǎn*	资产
Profit Margin	*yíng lì*	盈利
Advertisement	*guǎng gào*	广告
Deferred Payment	*yán qī fù kuǎn*	延期付款

Classified Vocabulary
Jī běn Cí huì
基 本 词 汇

Colours
yán sè
颜 色

Red	*Hóng sè*	红 色
Green	*lǜ sè*	绿 色
Blue	*lán sè*	蓝 色
Yellow	*huáng sè*	黄 色
White	*bái sè*	白 色
Black	*hēi sè*	黑 色
Purple	*zǐ sè*	紫 色
Saffron	*jú huáng sè*	橘 黄 色
Violet	*zǐ luó lán sè*	紫 罗 兰 色
Pink	*fěn hóng sè*	粉 红 色
Blue gray	*lán huī sè*	蓝 灰 色

Ash/Gray	*huī sè*	灰 色
Brown	*zōng sè*	棕 色
Silver	*yín sè*	银 色
Orange	*jú hóng sè*	橘 红 色
Golden	*jīnsè*	金 色

Trees
Zhí wù
植 物

Seed	*zhǒng zi*	种 子
Germ	*yòu yá*	幼 芽
Bud	*bài léi*	蓓 蕾
Root	*gēn xū*	根 须
Stem	*jìng gàn*	茎 干
Branch	*shù zhī*	树 枝
Trunk	*shù gàn*	树 干
Leaf	*shù yè*	树 叶

Fiber	*qiān wéi*	纤 维
Wood	*mù tou*	木 头
Gum	*shù zhī*	树 脂
Bamboo	*zhú zi*	竹 子
Tamarind	*luó wàng zi*	罗 望 子
Pine	*sōng shù*	松 树
Skin	*shù pí*	树 皮
Banyan	*róng shù*	榕 树
Acacia	*ā lā bó shù jiáo*	阿 拉 伯 树 胶
Teak	*yòu mù*	柚 木
Sandal	*tán xiāng shù*	檀 香 树
Cactus	*xiān rén zhǎng*	仙 人 掌
Oak	*xiàng shù*	橡 树
Lime tree	*pu tí shù*	菩 提 树
Mulbeery	*sāng shù*	桑 树
Walnut tree	*hú táo shù*	胡 桃 树
Palm	*zōng lǘ shù*	棕 榈 树

Flowers
Huā huì
花 卉

Azalea	*dù juān huā*	杜 鹃 花
Camellia	*shān chá huā*	山 茶 花
Crab apple	*hǎi táng huā*	海 棠 花
Chrysanthemum	*jú huā*	菊 花
Dahlia	*dà lì huā*	大 丽 花
Daffodil	*shuǐ xiān huā*	水 仙 花
Jasmine	*mó lì huā*	茉 莉 花
Lotus	*hé huā*	荷 花
Lily	*bǎi hé huā*	白 合 花
Magnolia	*yǔ lán huā*	玉 兰 花
Marigold	*jīn zhàn huā*	金 盏 花
Allspice	*là méi*	腊 梅
Dianna	*tán huā*	昙 花
Orchid	*lán huā*	兰 花

Peach blossom	*táo huā*	桃 花
Peony	*mu dān huā*	牡 丹 花
Plum blossom	*méi huā*	梅 花
Rose	*méi guì huā*	玫 瑰 花
Sunflower	*xiàng rì kuí*	向 日 葵
Tianthus	*shí zhú huā*	石 竹 花
Violet	*zǐ luó lán huā*	紫 罗 兰 花

Fruits
Guǒ shí
果 实

Walnut	*hú táo*	胡 桃
Cashewnut	*yāo guǒ*	腰 果
Raisin/Currant	*pú táo gān*	葡 萄 干
Date	*zǎo yē zi*	枣 椰 子
Pistachio	*kāi xīn guǒ*	开 心 果
Almond	*xìng rén*	杏 仁

Coconut	*yē zi*	椰 子
Apricot	*xìng zi*	杏 子
Apple	*píng guǒ*	苹 果
Banana	*xiāng jiāo*	香 蕉
Cherry	*yīng táo*	樱 桃
Mango	*máng guǒ*	芒 果
Peach	*táo zi*	桃 子
Grapes	*pú táo*	葡 萄
Watermelon	*xī guā*	西 瓜
Orange	*jú zi*	橘 子
Pear	*lí zi*	梨 子
Muskmelon	*xiāng guā*	香 瓜
Sugarcane	*gān zhè*	甘 蔗
Pineapple	*bō luó*	菠 萝
Lychee	*lī zhī*	荔 枝
Strawberry	*cǎo méi*	草 莓
Pomegranate	*shí līu*	石 榴

Guava	*fān shí līu*	番 石 榴
Plum	*lǐ zi*	李 子
Papaya	*mù guā*	木 瓜

Vegetables
Shū caì
蔬　菜

Potato	*tu dòu*	土 豆
Chinese cabbage	*dà bǎi cài*	大 白 菜
Cabbage	*yuán bǎi cài*	元 白 菜
Spinach	*bō cài*	菠 菜
Bamboo shoots	*sǔn zi*	笋 子
Cauliflower	*cài huā*	菜 花
Tomato	*xī hóng shì/ fān qié*	西 红 柿 / 蕃 茄
Lettuce	*wō sǔn*	莴 笋
Radish	*xiáo luó bù*	小 萝 卜
Carrot	*hú lúo bù*	胡 萝 卜

Turnip	*bǎi luó bù*	白 萝 卜
Brinjal	*qié zi*	茄 子
Garlic	*dà suàn*	大 蒜
Ginger	*jiāng*	姜
Parsley	*qíng cài*	芹 菜
Onion	*yáng cōng*	洋 葱
Mushroom	*mó gū*	蘑 菇
Beancurd	*dòu fu*	豆 腐
Bitter gourd	*ku guā*	苦 瓜
Beatroot	*hóng cài tóu*	红 菜 头
Beans	*dòu zi*	豆 子
Coriander	*xiāng cài*	香 菜
Cucumber	*huáng guā*	黄 瓜
Jackfruit	*mù bō luó*	木 菠 萝
Lemon	*níng méng*	柠 檬
Peas	*wān dòu*	豌 豆

Aquatic Products
Shuí chǎn
水 产

Hairtail fish	*dài yú*	带 鱼
Blackcarp fish	*qīng yú*	青 鱼
Silvercarp fish	*jí yú*	鲫 鱼
Pomfret fish	*sōng yú*	松 鱼
Salmon fish	*guì yú*	鲑 鱼
Cuttle fish	*mò yú*	墨 鱼
Sea cucumber	*hǎi shēn*	海 参
Shrimp	*xiā*	虾
Crab	*páng xiè*	螃 蟹
Prawn	*duì xiá*	对 虾
Turtle	*wū guī*	乌 龟
Sea weeds	*hǎi tái*	海 苔
Lobster	*lóng xiā*	龙 虾

Meat Products
Ròu zhì pǐn
肉 制 品

Beef	*níu ròu*	牛 肉
Mutton	*yáng ròu*	羊 肉
Pork	*zhū ròu*	猪 肉
Chicken	*jī ròu*	鸡 肉
Duck	*yā ròu*	鸭 肉
Fish meat	*yú ròu*	鱼 肉
Snake meat	*shé ròu*	蛇 肉
Ostrich meat	*tuó niǎo ròu*	驼 鸟 肉
Sausages	*xiāng cháng*	香 肠

Beverages
Yǐn liào
饮 料

Soft drinks	*qì shuǐ*	汽 水
Green tea	*lǜ chá*	绿 茶
Black tea	*hóng chá*	红 茶
Jasmine tea	*mó lì huā chá*	茉 莉 花 茶
Lemon tea	*níng méng chá*	柠 檬 茶
Instant coffee	*sù róng kā fēi*	速 溶 咖 啡
Black coffee	*kā fēi*	咖 啡
Cold coffee	*lěng kā fēi*	冷 咖 啡
Powdered milk	*nái fěn*	奶 粉
Condensed milk	*liàn ru*	炼 乳
Mineral water	*kuàng quán shuǐ*	矿 泉 水
Spring water	*quán shuǐ*	泉 水
Soda water	*sū dá shuǐ*	苏 打 水
Fruit juice	*guǒ zhī*	果 汁
Orange juice	jú zi zhī	橘 子 汁

Pineapple juice	*bō luó zhī*	菠 萝 汁
Tomato juice	*fān qié zhī*	蕃 茄 汁
Apple juice	*píng guǒ zhī*	苹 果 汁
Whisky	*wēi shì ji*	威 士 忌
Brandy	*bǎi lán dì*	白 兰 地
Cognac	*fǎ guó bǎi lán dì*	法 国 白 兰 地
Gin	*dù sōng zi jiǔ*	杜 松 子 酒
Vodka	*fú tè jiā jiǔ*	伏 特 加 酒
Cocktail	*jī wéi jiǔ*	鸡 尾 酒
Martini	*mǎ tí ní jiǔ*	马 提 尼 酒
White wine	*bǎi pú táo jiǔ*	白 葡 萄 酒
Red wine	*hóng pú táo jiǔ*	红 葡 萄 酒
Sherry	*xuě lì jiǔ*	雪 莉 酒
Champagne	*xiāng bīn jiǔ*	香 槟 酒
Maotai wine	*máo tái jiǔ*	茅 台 酒
Spirit	*bái jiǔ*	白 酒
Beer	*pí jiǔ*	啤 酒
Dry beer	*gān pí jiǔ*	干 啤 酒

Animals
Dòng wù
动 物

Alligator	*měi zhōu è yǘ*	美洲鳄鱼
Ant	*má yǐ*	蚂蚁
Bear	*xióng*	熊
Buffalo	*shuǐ níu*	水牛
Camel	*luò tuo*	骆驼
Cat	*māo*	猫
Cattle	*níu*	牛
Centipede	*wú gōng*	蜈蚣
Crane	*hè*	鹤
Crocodile	*è yǘ*	鳄鱼
Cow	*mu níu*	母牛
Deer	*lù*	鹿
Dog	*gǒu*	狗
Dolphin	*hǎi tún*	海豚

Dragon	*lóng*	龙
Eagle	*yīng*	鹰
Elephant	*xiàng*	象
Earthworm	*qīu yǐn*	蚯 蚓
Fox	*hú li*	狐 狸
Frog	*qīng wā*	青 蛙
Giraffe	*cháng jǐng lù*	长 颈 鹿
Gorilla	*dà xīng xing*	大 猩 猩
Horse	*mǎ*	马
Hippopotamus	*hé mǎ*	河 马
Jackal	*hú láng*	狐 狼
Kangaroo	*dài shu*	袋 鼠
Lion	*shī zi*	狮 子
Leopard	*měi zhōu bào*	美 洲 豹
Lizard	*xī yì*	蜥 蜴
Mongoose	*māo yòu*	猫 鼬
Mule	*luó*	骡

Monkey	*hóu zi*	猴 子
Ostrich	*tuó niǎo*	驼 鸟
Panda	*xióng māo*	熊 猫
Pig	*zhū*	猪
Rat	*shu*	鼠
Rabbit	*tù zi*	兔 子
Rhinoceros	*xī níu*	犀 牛
Scorpion	*xiē zi*	蝎 子
Sea lion	*hǎi shī*	海 狮
Seal	*hǎi bào*	海 豹
Shark	*shā yǘ*	鲨 鱼
Snake	*shé*	蛇
Sheep	*yáng*	羊
Snail	*wō níu*	蜗 牛
Spider	*zhī zhū*	蜘 蛛
Squirrel	*sōng shu*	松 鼠
Swan	*tiān é*	天 鹅

Tiger	*láo hu*	老虎
Turtle	*hǎi guī*	海龟
Ox	*huáng níu*	黄牛
Zebra	*bān ma*	斑马
Bee	*mì fēng*	蜜蜂
Butterfly	*hú dié*	蝴蝶
Crow	*wū yā*	乌鸦
Cuckoo	*bù gú niǎo*	布谷鸟
Dragonfly	*qīng tǐng*	蜻蜓
Dove	*gē zi*	鸽子
Drone	*xióng fēng*	雄蜂
Duck	*yā zi*	鸭子
Fly	*cāng yīng*	苍蝇
Grasshopper	*zhà měng*	蚱蜢
Goose	*é*	鹅
Hen	*mu jī*	母鸡
Mosquito	*wén zi*	蚊子

Owl	*māo tóu yīng*	猫 头 鹰
Peacock	*kǒng què*	孔 雀
Penguin	*qǐ é*	企 鹅
Parrot	*yīng wū*	鹦 鹉
Pigeon	*gē zi*	鸽 子
Sea gull	*hǎi ōu*	海 鸥
Sparrow	*má què*	麻 雀
Wood-pecker	*zhuó mù niǎo*	啄 木 鸟

Body Parts
Rén tǐ
人 体

Head	*tóu*	头
Forehead	*é tóu*	额 头
Hair	*tóu fà*	头 发
Scull	*tóu gu*	头 骨

Brain	*dà nǎo*	大 脑
Eye	*yǎn jīng*	眼 睛
Eyelid	*méi máo*	眉 毛
Eyeball	*yǎn qíu*	眼 球
Ear	*ěr*	耳
Lip	*zuǐ chún*	嘴唇
Nose	*bí zi*	鼻 子
Cheek	*miàn jiá*	面 颊
Tongue	*shé tóu*	舌 头
Face	*liǎn*	脸
Jaw	*xià è*	下 颚
Teeth	*yá chǐ*	牙 齿
Gum	*yá yín*	牙 龈
Mouth	*zuǐ*	嘴
Chin	*xià bā*	下 巴
Beard	*hú xū*	胡 须
Throat	*hóu*	喉

Neck	*jǐng*	颈
Collarbone	*suó gu*	锁 骨
Shoulder	*jiān*	肩
Chest	*xiōng bù*	胸 部
Lung	*fèi*	肺
Heart	*xīn zàng*	心 脏
Blood	*xuě yè*	血 液
Artery	*dòng mài*	动 脉
Muscle	*jī ròu*	肌 肉
Windpipe	*qì guǎn*	气 管
Breast	*ru fáng*	乳 房
Rib	*lēi gu*	肋 骨
Back	*bèi*	背
Spine	*jí zhuī gu*	脊 椎 骨
Upper arm	*shàng bì*	上 臂
Elbow	*zhǒu*	肘
Waist	*yāo*	腰

Abdomen	*fù bù*	腹 部
Intestine	*cháng*	肠
Kidney	*shèn*	肾
Liver	*gān zàng*	肝 脏
Uterus	*zǐ gōng*	子 宫
Gallbladder	*dǎn náng*	胆 囊
Urinary bladder	*páng guāng*	膀 胱
Nerve	*shén jīng*	神 经
Fore arm	*qián bì*	前 臂
Navel	*dù qí*	肚 脐
Thumb	*mú zhǐ*	拇 指
Index finger	*shí zhǐ*	食 指
Middle finger	*zhōng zhǐ*	中 指
Ring finger	*wú míng zhǐ*	无 名 指
Little finger	*xiáo zhǐ*	小 指
Palm	*shóu zhǎng*	手 掌
Wrist	*wǎn*	腕

Hand	*shǒu*	手
Finger nail	*zhı jia*	指 甲
Buttocks	*tún bù*	臀 部
Pelvis	*gu pén*	骨 盆
Leg	*tuǐ*	腿
Thigh	*dà tuǐ*	大 腿
Thigh bone	*dà tuǐ gu*	大 腿 骨
Knee	*xī gài*	膝 盖
Knee cap	*xī gài gu*	膝 盖 骨
Lower leg	*xiáo tuǐ gu*	小 腿 骨
Calf	*xiǎo tuǐ dù*	小 腿 肚
Ankle	*huái*	踝
Instep	*jiǎo bèi*	脚 背
Sole of the foot	*jiáo zhǎng*	脚 掌
Toe	*jiáo zhǐ*	脚 趾
Heel	*jiǎo hòu gēn*	脚 后 跟

Clothes & Garments
Yī liào jí fú zhuāng

衣料 及 服 装

Shirt	*chèn shān*	衬 衫
Tie	*lǐng dài*	领 带
Bow	*lǐng jié*	领 结
Coat	*shàng yī*	上 衣
Waistcoat	*bèi xīn*	背 心
Overcoat	*dà yī*	大 衣
Raincoat	*yǔ yī*	雨 衣
Jacket	*jiá kè shān*	夹 克 衫
Sweater	*máo yī*	毛 衣
Suit	*xī zhuāng*	西 装
Gown	*cháng wài yī*	长 外 衣
Wedding gown	*hūn shā*	婚 纱
Blouse	*nǚ shì chén shān*	女 式 衬 衫
T-shirt	*hàn shān*	汗 衫
Scarf	*tóu jīn*	头 巾

Muffler	*wéi jīn*	围 巾
Hat	*mào zi*	帽 子
Button	*nǐu kòu*	钮 扣
Trousers	*kù zi*	裤 子
Shorts	*duǎn kù*	短 裤
Sportswear	*yùn dòng fú*	运 动 服
Pocket	*kǒu dài*	口 袋
Belt	*pí dài*	皮 带
Handkerchief	*shǒu pà*	手 帕
Napkin	*cān jīn*	餐 巾
Gloves	*shǒu tào*	手 套
Sleeve	*xìu zi*	袖 子
Skirt	*qún zi*	裙 子
Stocking	*cháng wà*	长 袜
Underwear	*nèi yī*	内 衣
Diaper	*niào bù*	尿 布
Towel	*máo jīn*	毛 巾

Apron	*wéi qún*	围裙
Leather shoes	*pí xié*	皮鞋
Cloth shoes	*bù xié*	布鞋
Shoelace	*xié dài*	鞋带
Blanket	*tǎn zi*	毯子
Canvas	*fán bù*	帆布
Cushion	*yǐ diàn*	椅垫
Cushion cover	*yǐ diàn tào*	椅垫套
Bedsheet	*chuáng dān*	床单
Quilt	*mián bèi*	棉被
Quilt cover	*bèi tào*	被套
Pillow	*zhěn tóu*	枕头
Pillow cover	*zhěn tóu tào*	枕头套

Jewels & Ornaments
Bǎo shí yu Zhuāng shì pǐn
宝 石 与 装 饰 品

Cat's eye	*māo yǎn*	猫 眼
Coral	*shān hú*	珊 瑚
Diamond	*zuàn shí*	钻 石
Emerald	*lǜ bǎo shí*	绿 宝 石
Opal	*dàn bǎi shí*	蛋 白 石
Real pearl	*zhēn zhū*	珍 珠
Cultured pearl	*zhēn zhū*	珍 珠
Ruby	*hóng bǎo shí*	红 宝 石
Sapphire	*lán bǎo shí*	蓝 宝 石
Turquoise	*lǜ sōng shí*	绿 松 石
Zircon	*gào shí*	锆 石
Ring	*jiè zhǐ*	戒 指
Bracelet/Bangle	*shǒu zhuó*	手 镯
Ear-ring	*ěr huán*	耳 环
Nose-pin	*bí huán*	鼻 环

Pendant	*xiàng liàn zhùi zǐ*	项 链 坠 子
Chain	*xiàng quān*	项 圈
Necklace	*xiàng liàn*	项 链

Musical Instruments & Terms
Yuè qì jí Yīn yuè Míng chēng
乐 器 及 音 乐 名 称

Drum	*gu*	鼓
Bugle	*hào*	号
Piano	*gāng qín*	钢 琴
Flute	*cháng dí*	长 笛
Violin	*xiǎo tí qín*	小 提 琴
Bagpipe	*fēng dí*	风 笛
Clarinet	*dān huáng guǎn*	单 簧 管
Guitar	*jí tā*	吉 他
Harmonium	*hé shēng*	和 声

Bell	*líng*	铃
Accordion	*shōu fēng qín*	手风琴
Saxophone	*sà kè sī guǎn*	萨克斯管
Harp	*shù qín*	竖琴
Mouth organ	*kǒu fēng qín*	口风琴
Xylophone	*mù qín*	木琴
National Anthem	*guó gē*	国歌
Concert	*yīng yuè huì*	音乐会
Composer	*zuó qu jiā*	作曲家
Orchestra	*guǎn xiān yuè duì*	管弦乐队
Classical music	*gú diǎn yīn yuè*	古典音乐
Pop music	*líu xíng yīn yuè*	流行音乐
Light music	*qīng yīn yuè*	轻音乐
Folk music	*xīang cūn yīn yuè*	乡村音乐
Rock-n-roll	*yáo gun yuè*	摇滚乐
Solo	*dú zòu*	独奏
Recital	*dú chàng huì*	独唱会

Audience	*tīng zhòng*	听 众
Makeup room	*hòu tái*	后 台
Announcer	*bào mù yuán*	报 幕 员
Dancer	*wú dǎo yǎn yuán*	舞 蹈 演 员
Singer	*gē chàng yǎn yuán*	歌 唱 演 员
Director	*dáo yǎn*	导 演
Actor	*nán yǎn yuán*	男 演 员
Actress	*nǚ yǎn yuán*	女 演 员

Household Articles
Jiā tǐng wù pǐn
家 庭 物 品

Wardrobe	*yī guì*	衣 柜
Mirror	*jìng zi*	镜 子
Curtain	*chuāng lián*	窗 帘
Electric fan	*diàn shàn*	电 扇
Clock	*zhōng*	钟

Dressing-table	*shū zhuāng tái*	梳 妆 台
Lamp	*tái dēng*	台 灯
Carpet	*dì tǎn*	地 毯
Dining table	*fàn zhuō*	饭 桌
Tea-tray	*chá pán*	茶 盘
Tea set	*chá jù*	茶 具
Tea-pot	*chá hú*	茶 壶
Sofa	*shā fā*	沙 发
Refrigerator	*diàn bīng xiāng*	电 冰 箱
Electric iron	*diàn yùn dǒu*	电 熨 斗
Cosmetic	*huà zhuāng pǐn*	化 妆 品
Comb	*shū zi*	梳 子
Lipstick	*chún gāo*	唇 膏
Mosquito net	*wén zhàng*	蚊 帐
Bedding	*chuáng shàng yòng pǐn*	床 上 用 品
Dinner set	*cān jù*	餐 具
Knife	*dāo zi*	刀 子

Fork	*chā zi*	叉子
Spoon	*sháo zi*	勺子
Cupboard	*wǎn dié chú*	碗揲橱
Pressure cooker	*gāo yà guō*	高压锅
Broom	*sào zhǒu*	扫帚
Washing machine	*xǐ yī jī*	洗衣机
Wash basin	*guàn xǐ chí*	盥洗池
Sink	*xí dí cáo*	洗涤槽
Brush	*shuā zi*	刷子
Razor	*guā hú dāo*	刮胡刀
Toothpaste	*yá gāo*	牙膏
Toothbrush	*yá shuā*	牙刷
Soap	*féi zào*	肥皂
Toilet-roll	*shóu zhǐ*	手纸
Detergent	*xǐ yī fěn*	洗衣粉
Bathtub	*yù chí*	浴池
Bucket	*tǒng*	桶
Lock	*suǒ*	锁

Oven	*kǎo xiāng*	烤 箱
Candle	*là zhú*	蜡 烛
Needle	*zhēn*	针
Thread	*xiàn*	线
Sewing machine	*féng rèn jī*	缝 纫 机

Professions
zhí yè
职 业

Architect	*jiàn zhù shī*	建 筑 师
Journalist	*jì zhě*	记 者
Teacher	*jiào shī*	教 师
Judge	*fǎ guān*	法 官
Lawyer	*lǜ shī*	律 师
Engineer	*gōng chéng shī*	工 程 师
Designer	*shè jì shī*	设 计 师
Banker	*yín háng jiā*	银 行 家

Doctor	*yī shēng*	医生
Contractor	*chéng bāo shāng*	承包商
Publisher	*chū bǎn shāng*	出版商
Photographer	*shè yǐng shī*	摄影师
Accountant	*kuài jì shī*	会计师
Writer	*zuò jiā*	作家
Editor	*biān jí*	编辑
Farmer	*nóng mín*	农民
Magician	*mó shù shī*	魔术师
Weaver	*zhī bù gōng*	织布工
Shoe-maker	*xié jiàng*	鞋匠
Jeweller	*zhū bǎo shāng*	珠宝商
Tailor	*cái fèng*	裁缝
Baker	*miàn bāo shī*	面包师
Chemist	*yào jì shī*	药剂师
Cook	*chú zi*	厨子
Blacksmith	*tiě jiàng*	铁匠

Goldsmith	*jīn jiàng*	金 匠
Barber	*lǐ fà shī*	理 发 师
Painter	*huà jiā*	画 家
Sweeper	*qīng jié gōng*	清 洁 工
Gardener	*yuán dīng*	园 丁
Fisherman	*yú fū*	渔 夫
Carpenter	*mù jiàng*	木 匠
Watchman	*kàn shóu zhě*	看 守 者
Nurse	*hù shī*	护 士
Mason	*shí jiàng*	石 匠
Postman	*yóu chǎi*	邮 差
Plumber	*guǎn dào gōng*	管 道 工
Driver	*sī jī*	司 机
Navigator	*lǐng hǎng yuán*	领 航 员
Cartoonist	*màn huà jiā*	漫 画 家
Dancer	*wú nǚ*	舞 女
Commentator	*jiě shuō yuán*	解 说 员

Announcer	*bō yīn yuán*	播 音 员
Politician	*zhèng kè*	政 客
Policeman	*jǐng guān*	警 官
Salesman	*tuī xiāo yuán*	推 销 员
Manager	*jīng lǐ*	经 理
Clerk	*zhí yuán*	职 员

Spices
Xiāng liào
香 料

Pepper	*hú jiāo*	胡 椒
Cardamon	*xiǎo dòu kòu*	小 豆 寇
Saffron	*zàng hóng huā*	藏 红 花
Nutmeg	*ròu dòu kòu*	肉 豆 寇
Cumin	*xiǎo huí xiāng*	小 茴 香
Cinnamon	*guì pí*	桂 皮

Salt	*yán*	盐
Red Chilly	*hóng là jiāo*	红 辣 椒
Cloves	*dīng xiāng*	丁 香
Dry Ginger	*gān jiāng*	干 姜
Aniseeds	*dà liào*	大 料
Turmeric	*jiāng huáng*	姜 黄
Asafetida	*a wèi jiāo*	阿 魏 胶

Office Appliances
Bàn gōng yòng pǐn
办 公 用 品

Switch Board	*diàn huà jiāo huàn jī*	电 话 交 换 机
Table Calendar	*tái lì*	台 历
File	*wén jiàn*	文 件
Thumb Tack	*tú dīng*	图 钉
Paper Clip	*qū biē zhēn*	曲 别 针

Glue	*jiāo shuǐ*	胶 水
Paper Cutter	*cái zhǐ dāo*	裁 纸 刀
Note Pad	*jì shì běn*	记 事 本
Diary	*rì jì*	日 记
Ball Pen	*yuán zhū bǐ*	圆 珠 笔
Fountain Pen	*gāng bǐ*	钢 笔
Pencil	*qiān bǐ*	铅 笔
Marker	*jì hào bǐ*	记 号 笔
Sharpener	*xiāo bǐ dāo*	削 笔 刀
Eraser	*xiàng pí cā*	橡 皮 擦
Stapler	*dìng shū jī*	钉 书 机
Seal	*tú zhāng*	图 章
Ink Pad	*yın tái*	印 台
Scale	*chǐ zi*	尺 子
Desk	*shū zhuō*	书 桌
Revolving Chair	*zhuàn yǐ*	转 椅
Waste Paper Basket	*zì zhǐ lōu*	字 纸 篓

Type Writer	*dǎ zì jī*	打子机
Computer	*jì suàn jī*	计算机
Telephone	*diàn huà*	电话
Briefcase	*gōng wén bāo*	公文包
Pen Stand	*bǐ jià*	笔架
Table Lamp	*tái dēng*	台灯
Calculator	*jì suàn qì*	计算器
Stencil	*là bǎn*	蜡板
Paper Weight	*zhèn zhǐ*	镇纸
Letter Head	*xìn tóu*	信头
File Cabinet	*wén jiàn guì*	文件柜
Sealing Wax	*huó kǒu qí*	火口漆
Visitor's Book	*lái kè dēng jì bù*	来客登记簿
Typing Paper	*dǎ yìn zhǐ*	打印纸
Carbon Paper	*fù xiě zhǐ*	复写纸
Sand Paper	*shā zhǐ*	砂纸
Graph Paper	*zuò biāo zhǐ*	坐标纸

Art Paper	*tóng bán zhǐ*	铜 板 纸
Compass	*zhǐ nán zhēn*	指 南 针

Transport & Communication
Jiāo tōng yùn shū
交 通 运 输

Fire extinguisher	*miè huǒ qì*	灭 火 器
Cycle	*zì xíng chē*	自 行 车
Horse cart	*mǎ chē*	马 车
Bulldozer	*duī tu jī*	堆 土 机
Motorcycle	*mó tuō chē*	摩 托 车
Car	*qì chē*	汽 车
Tram	*yǒu guǐ diàn chē*	有 轨 电 车
Trolley Bus	*wú guǐ diàn chē*	无 轨 电 车
Truck	*huǒ chē*	货 车
Three Wheeler	*sān lún chē*	三 轮 车

Jeep	*jí pu chē*	吉 普 车
Tractor	*tuō lā jī*	拖 拉 机
Bus	*gōng gòng qì chē*	公 共 汽 车
Van	*miàn bāo chē*	面 包 车
Train	*huǒ chē*	火 车
Fire Engine	*jìu huǒ chē*	救 火 车
Rickshaw	*rén lì sān lún chē*	人 力 三 轮 车
Crane	*qǐ zhòng jī*	起 重 机
Boat	*xiǎo chuán*	小 船
Motor Boat	*mó tuō tǐng*	摩 托 艇
Oil Tanker	*shū yóu chuán*	输 油 船
Ship	*chuán*	船
Rowing Boat	*shān bǎn*	舢 板
Yacht	*yóu tǐng*	游 艇
Life Boat	*jìu shēng tǐng*	救 生 艇
Aeroplane	*fēi jī*	飞 机
Cargoplane	*huò jī*	货 机
Trainer plane	*kè jī*	客 机

Glider	*huá xiáng jī*	滑 翔 机
Helicopter	*zhí shēng jī*	直 升 机
Jet	*pēn qì jī*	喷 气 机
Parachute	*jiàng luò sǎn*	降 落 伞

Military Terms
Jūn shì míng chéng
军 事 名 称

Army	*lù jūn*	陆 军
Airforce	*kōng jūn*	空 军
Navy	*hǎi jūn*	海 军
Marine	*hǎi jūn* *lù zhàn duí*	海 军 陆 战 队
Anti-chemical corps	*fáng huà bù duì*	防 化 部 队
Soldier	*zhàn shì*	战 士
Sailor	*shuǐ bīng*	水 兵
Airman	*fēi xíng yuán*	飞 行 员

Paratrooper	*sǎn bīng*	伞 兵
Fighter pilot	*zhàn dòu jī* *jià shǐ yuán*	战 斗 机 架 驶 员
Militia	*mín bīng*	民 兵
Engineering corps	*gōng chéng bù duì*	工 程 部 队
Rear services units	*hòu qín bù duì*	后 勤 部 队
Ordinance depot	*jūn xiè kù*	军 械 库
Brigade	*lǚ*	旅
Regiment	*lián duì*	联 队
Military Region	*jūn qū*	军 区
Military base	*jūn shì jī dì*	军 事 基 地
Military exercise	*jūn shì yǎn xí*	军 事 演 习
Military uniform	*jūn zhuāng*	军 装
Weapon	*wu qì*	武 器
Cartridge	*zǐ dàn*	子 弹
Shell	*dàn ké*	弹 壳
Ammunition	*dàn yào*	弹 药
Magazine	*dàn xiá*	弹 匣

Radar	*léi dá*	雷 达
Tank	*tǎn kè*	坦 克
Pistol	*shǒu qiāng*	手 枪
Automatic rifle	*zì dòng bù qiāng*	自 动 步 枪
Light machine gun	*qīng jī qiāng*	轻 机 枪
Anti-aircraft gun	*gāo shè jī qiāng*	高 射 机 枪
Anti-tank gun	*fán tǎn kè pào*	反 坦 克 炮
Grenade	*shǒu líu dàn*	手 榴 弹
Mine	*dì léi*	地 雷
Torpedo	*yú léi*	鱼 雷
Mortar	*pò jī pào*	迫 击 炮
Rocket launcher	*huǒ jiàn fā shè qì*	火 箭 发 射 器
Howitzer	*líu dàn pào*	榴 弹 炮
Reconnaissance plane	*zhēn chá jī*	侦 察 机
Fighter	*zhàn dòu jī*	战 斗 机
Bomber	*hōng zhà jī*	轰 炸 机
Stealth bomber	*yǐn xíng hōng zhà jī*	隐 形 轰 炸 机

Aircraft carrier	*háng kōng mu jiàn*	航 空 母 舰
Cruiser	*xún yáng jiàn*	巡 洋 舰
Submarine	*qián tǐng*	潜 艇
Air-to-air missile	*kōng kōng dǎo dàn*	空 空 导 弹
Air-to-ground missile	*kōng dì dǎo dàn*	空 地 导 弹
Anti-ballistic Missile	*fǎn dàn dào dǎo dàn*	反 弹 道 导 弹
Missile launcher	*dǎo dàn fā shè qì*	导弹发射器
Atomic weapon	*yuán zi wǔ qì*	原 子 武 器
Nuclear weapon	*hé wǔ qì*	核 武 器
Nuclear warhead	*hé dàn tóu*	核 弹 头
Convential weapons	*cháng guī wǔ qì*	常 规 武 器
Intermedium Range Ballistic Missile (IRBM)	*zhōng chéng dàn dào dǎo dàn*	中 程 弹 道 导 弹
Multiple Independently Ballistic Missile (MIRV)	*duō dàn tóu dàn dào dǎo dàn*	多 弹 头 弹 道 导 弹
Inter-Continental Ballistic Missile (ICBM)	*zhōu jì dàn dào dǎo dàn*	洲 际 弹 道 导 弹

Geography
Dì lǐ
地 理

Map	*dì tú*	地 图
Earthquake	*dì zhèn*	地 震
Seaquake	*hǎi zhèn*	海 震
Avalanche	*xǔe bēng*	雪 崩
Volcano	*huǒ shān*	火 山
Glacier	*bīng hé*	冰 河
Iceberg	*bīng shān*	冰 山
Gulf	*hǎi wān*	海 湾
Island	*dǎo yu*	岛 屿
Peninsula	*bàn dǎo*	半 岛
Waterfall	*pù bù*	瀑 布
Spring	*wēn quán*	温 泉
Well	*jǐng*	井
Highland	*gāo dì*	高 地

Plateau	*gāo yuán*	高原
Plain	*píng yuán*	平原
Delta	*sān jiǎo zhōu*	三角洲

Sports
Tǐ yù
体育

Hockey	*qū gùn qíu*	曲棍球
Cricket	*bǎn qíu*	板球
Football	*zú qíu*	足球
Basketball	*lán qíu*	蓝球
Volleyball	*pái qíu*	排球
Tennis	*wǎng qíu*	网球
Table-Tennis	*pīng pāng qíu*	乒乓球
Badminton	*yu máo qíu*	羽毛球
Baseball	*bàng qíu*	棒球
Handball	*shǒu qíu*	手球

Gymnastics	*tǐ cāo*	体 操
Swimming	*yóu yǒng*	游 泳
Freestyle	*zì yóu yǒng*	自 由 泳
Breast-stroke	*wā yǒng*	蛙 泳
Butterfly-stroke	*dié yǒng*	蝶 泳
Back-stroke	*yáng yǒng*	仰 泳
Diving	*tiào shuǐ*	跳 水
Skiing	*huá shuǐ*	滑 水
Ice skating	*huá bīng*	滑 冰
Roller skating	*hàn bīng*	旱 冰
Figure skating	*huā yàng* *huá bīng*	花 样 滑 冰
Martial arts	*wǔ shù*	武 术
Track and field	*tián jìng*	田 径
Sprint	*duán pǎo*	短 跑
Marathon	*mǎ lā sōng*	马 拉 松
Relay	*jiē lì*	接 力
Hurdles	*zhàng ài sài*	障 碍 赛

High jump	*tìao gāo*	跳 高
Long jump	*tìao yuǎn*	跳 远
Shot-put	*qiān qíu*	铅 球
Discus	*tíe bǐng*	铁 饼
Javelin throw	*biāo qiāng*	标 枪
Polo	*má qíu*	马 球
Water polo	*shuǐ qíu*	水 球
Golf	*gāo ěr fū qíu*	高 尔 夫 球
Fencing	*jī jìan*	击 剑
Wrestling	*shuāi jiāo*	摔 跤
Shooting	*shè jī*	射 击
Windsurfing	*fān bǎn*	帆 板
Billiards	*tái qíu(mei shi)*	台球（美式）
Snooker	*tái qíu(ying shi)*	台球（英式）
Court	*qıu chǎng*	球 场
Stand	*kàn tái*	看 台
Stadium	*yùn dòng chǎng*	运 动 场

Match	*bǐ sài*	比 赛
Score	*bǐ fēn*	比 分
Team	*duì*	队
Referee	*cái pàn*	裁 判
Indoor games	*shì nèi yùn dòng*	室 内 运 动
Olympics	*ào yùn huì*	奥 运 会
Asian games	*yà yùn huì*	亚 运 会
League	*lián sài*	联 赛
Championship	*jǐn biāo sài*	锦 标 赛
Quater-final	*sì fēn zhī* *yī jué sài*	四 分 之 一 决 赛
Semi-final	*bàn jué sài*	半 决 赛
Final	*jué sài*	决 赛
Champion	*guàn jūn*	冠 军
Runners up	*yà jūn*	亚 军
Win	*yíng*	赢
Lose	*shū*	输

Art & Culture
Wén huà yì shù
文 化 艺 术

Library	*tú shū guǎn*	图 书 馆
Librarian	*tú shū guǎn guán lǐ yuán*	图 书 馆 管 理 员
Book	*shū*	书
Bookshelf	*shū jià*	书 架
Pictorial	*huà bào*	画 报
Magazine	*zá zhì*	杂 志
Reading room	*yué lǎn shì*	阅 览 室
Brush	*huà bǐ*	画 笔
Drawing board	*huà jià*	画 架
Sculpture	*diāo kě*	雕 刻
Ivory carving	*xiàng yá diāo kè*	象 牙 雕 刻
Wood cutting	*mù kè*	木 刻
Statue	*diāo xiàng*	雕 像
Portrait	*xiāo xiàng*	肖 像

Poster	*zhāo tiē*	招 贴
Calligraphy	*shū fǎ*	书 法
Antique	*gú dǒng*	古 董
Masterpiece	*míng zhù*	名 著
Relics	*yí wù*	遗 物
Pottery	*táo qì*	陶 器

Photography & Films
Shè yǐng hé Diàn yǐng
摄 影 和 电 影

Lens	*tòu jìng*	透 镜
Flashlight	*shǎn guāng dēng*	闪 光 灯
Camera	*zhào xiàng jī*	照 相 机
Camera battery	*zhào xiàng jī diàn chí*	照 相 机 电 池
Binoculars	*wàng yuǎn jìng*	望 远 镜
Projector	*fàng yǐng jī*	放 映 机

Amplifier	*fàng dà jī*	放大机
Screen	*yín mù*	银幕
Satellite transmission	*wèi xīng zhuǎn bō*	卫星转播
Movie camera	*shè xiàng jī*	摄像机
Three-dimensional	*sān wéi*	三维
Newsreel	*xīn wén jì lù piān*	新闻记录片
Documentary	*zhuān tī piān*	专题片
Cartoon film	*dòng huà piān*	动画片
Dubbing	*yì zhì piān*	译制片
Drama	*xì jù*	戏剧
Skit	*huó bào jù*	活报剧
Comedy	*xǐ jù*	喜剧
Tragedy	*bēi jù*	悲剧
Puppet show	*mù ǒu xì*	木偶戏
Threater	*xì yuàn*	戏院
Cinema	*diàn yǐng*	电影

Electronics & Electrical Equipments
Diàn zi hé Dian qì
电 子 和 电 器

Television	*diàn shì*	电 视
Radio	*shōu yīn jī*	收 音 机
Tape-recorder	*lù yīn jī*	录 音 机
Record-player	*diàn chàng jī*	电 唱 机
Music-system	*yīn xiǎng xì tǒng*	音 响 系 统
Microphone	*mài kè fēng*	麦 克 风
Earphone	*ěr jī*	耳 机
Loudspeaker	*yáng shēng qì*	扬 声 器
Stereo	*lì tǐ shēng*	立 体 声
Cassette	*cí dài*	磁 带
Video tape	*lù xiàng dài*	录 像 带
Audio C.D.	*yīn yuè guāng pán*	音 乐 光 盘
Video C.D.	*diàn yǐng guāng pán*	电 影 光 盘

Air-conditioner	*kōng tiáo jī*	空 调 机
Washing machine	*xǐ yī jī*	洗 衣 机
Refrigerator	*diàn bīng xiāng*	电 冰 箱
Electric hair drier	*diàn chuī fēng*	电 吹 风
Vacuum cleaner	*xī chén qì*	洗 尘 器
Pump	*cōu shuǐ jī*	抽 水 机
Electric heater	*diàn lú*	电 炉
Generator	*fā diàn jī*	发 电 机
Picture tube	*xiǎn xiàng guǎn*	显 像 管
Plug	*chā tóu*	插 头
Socket	*chā zuò*	插 座
Switch	*kāi guān*	开 关
Fuse box	*diàn zhá hé*	电 闸 盒
Thermostat	*héng wēn qì*	恒 温 器
Transistor	*jīn tí guǎn*	晶 体 管
Resistor	*diàn zu qì*	电 阻 器
Convertor	*wěn yā qì*	稳 压 器
Semi-Conductor	*bàn dáo tǐ*	半 导 体

Integrated Circuit	*jí chéng diàn lù*	集 成 电 路
Armature	*diàn shū*	电 枢
Voltmeter	*diàn biǎo*	电 表
Diode	*èr jí guǎn*	二 极 管
Triode	*sān jí guǎn*	三 极 管
Meter band	*bō duàn*	波 段
Wave length	*bō cháng*	波 长
Mhz	*zhào hè*	兆 赫
Khz	*qiān hè*	千 赫
Input	*shū rù*	输 入
Output	*shū chū*	输 出
Electrode	*diàn jiě*	电 解
Short circuit	*duǎn lù*	短 路
Ampere	*ān péi*	安 培
Ohm	*ōu mu*	欧 姆
Watt	*wǎ tè*	瓦 特
kWh	*qiān wǎ/xiǎo shí*	千 瓦/小 时
Horsepower	*mǎ lì*	马 力

Mineral & Metals
Kuàng shí jí Jīn shu
矿 石 及 金 属

Raw meterial	*yuán liào*	原 料
Reserves	*chu cáng liàng*	储 藏 量
Stone	*shí*	石
Ore	*kuàng shí*	矿 石
Marble	*dà lǐ shí*	大 理 石
Flint	*sùi shí*	燧 石
Mica	*yún mu*	云 母
Carbon	*tàn*	碳
Coal	*méi tàn*	煤 炭
Coal pit	*méi tàn kuàng jǐng*	煤 炭 矿 井
Lignite	*huò méi*	祸 煤
Chalk	*fěn*	粉
Sulfur	*líu huáng*	硫 磺
Ferrous metals	*hēi sè jīn shu*	黑 色 金 属

Non-ferrous metals	*yǒu sè jīn shu*	有 色 金 属
Zinc	*xīn*	锌
Tin	*xī*	锡
Antimony	*tī*	锑
Lead	*qiān*	铅
Gold	*jīn*	金
Silver	*yín*	银
Copper	*tóng*	铜
Bronze	*huáng tóng*	黄 铜
Bell-metal	*qīng tóng*	青 铜
Iron	*tiě*	铁
Pig iron	*shēng tiě*	生 铁
Wrought iron	*shú tiě*	熟 铁
Steel	*gāng*	钢
Alloy steel	*hé jīn gāng*	合 金 钢
Spring steel	*dán huǎng gāng*	弹 簧 钢
Stainless steel	*bú xìu gāng*	不 锈 钢
Steel billet	*gāng pī*	钢 坯

Rolled steel	*zhá cái*	轧 材
Mercury	*shuǐ yín*	水 银
Magnet	*cí tiě*	磁 铁
Foundry	*zhù zào*	铸 造
Casting	*zhù jiàn*	铸 件
Moulding	*mó zhì*	模 制
Die	*yìng mó*	硬 模
Blast furnace	*gāo lú*	高 炉
Smelting Plant	*yě liàn chǎng*	冶 炼 厂
Hydraulic press	*shuǐ yā jī*	水 压 机
Oxidizing agent	*yǎng huà jì*	氧 化 剂
Catalyst	*cuī huà zuò yòng*	催 化 作 用

Oil & Gas
Shí yóu Tiān rán qì
石 油 天 然 气

Marine deposit	*hǎi xiàng chén jí*	海 相 沉 积

Continental deposit	*lù xiàng chén jí*	陆相沉积
Offshore oilfield	*hǎi shàng yóu tián*	海上油田
Oil layer	*yóu céng*	油层
Oil well	*yóu jǐng*	油井
Oil reserve	*chu yóu liàng*	储油量
Oil storage	*yóu kù*	油库
Crude oil	*yuán yóu*	原油
Oil refinery	*liàn yóu chǎng*	炼油厂
Oil tanker	*yóu guàn*	油罐
Pipe line	*shū yóu guǎn*	输油管
Drilling	*zuàn jǐng*	钻井
Pumping station	*yóu bèng fáng*	油泵房
Gas field	*qì tián*	气田
Natural gas	*tiān rán qì*	天然气
Cracked gas	*liè huà qì*	裂化气
Diesel oil	*chái yóu*	柴油
Fuel oil	*rán liào yóu*	燃料油
Kerosene	*méi yóu*	煤油

Engine oil	*jī yóu*	机 油
Break oil	*shā chē yóu*	刹 车 油
Lubricant	*rùn huá yóu*	润 滑 油

Chemicals
Huà xué pǐn
化 学 品

Hydrogen (H)	*qīng*	氢
Helium (He)	*hài*	氦
Lithium (Li)	*lǐ*	锂
Beryllium (Be)	*pō*	铍
Carbon (N)	*tàn*	碳
Nitrogen (N)	*dàn*	氮
Oxygen (O)	*yǎng*	氧
Fluorine (F)	*fú*	氟
Sodium (Na)	*nà*	钠
Magnesium (Mg)	*yǎng huà měi*	氧 化 镁

Aluminium (Al)	*fán tu*	矾 土
Silicon (Si)	*xī*	矽
Phosphorus (P)	*lín*	磷
Sulfur (S)	*líu*	硫
Chlorine (Cl)	*lú*	氯
Potassium (K)	*jiǎ*	钾
Calcium (Ca)	*gài*	钙
Titanium (Ti)	*tài*	钛
Manganese (Mn)	*mèng*	锰
Iron (Fe)	*tiě*	铁
Nickel (Ni)	*níe*	镍
Copper (Cu)	*tóng*	铜
Zinc (Zn)	*xīn*	锌
Silver (Ag)	*yín*	银
Tin (Sn)	*xī*	锡
Antimony (Sb)	*tī*	锑
Iodine (I)	*diǎn*	碘
Gold (Au)	*jīn*	金

Mercury (Hg)	*shuǐ yín*	水 银
Lead (Pb)	*qiān*	铅
Radium (Ra)	*léi*	镭
Uranium (U)	*yòu*	铀
Plutonium (Pu)	*bù*	钚
Germanium (Ge)	*zhě*	锗
Bromine (Br)	*xìu*	溴
Barium (Ba)	*bèi*	钡
Thallium (Tl)	*tuó*	铊
Wolfram (W)	*wū*	钨
Phosphoric Acid	*lín suān*	磷 酸
Zinc Phosphate	*lín suān xīn*	磷 酸 锌
Activated Carbon	*huó xìng tàn*	活 性 炭
Polyethylene	*jú yǐ xī*	聚 乙 烯
Calcium Carbonate	*qīng zhì tàn suān gài*	轻 质 碳 酸 钙
Calcium Chloride	*lú huà gài*	氯 化 钙
Potassium Chlorate	*lú suān jiǎ*	氯 酸 钾

Sodium Nitrate	*xiā suān nà*	硝 酸 钠
Citric Acid	*níng méng suān*	柠 檬 酸
Zinc Oxide (Zno)	*yǎng huà xīn*	氧 化 锌
Terpineol	*sōng yóu chún*	松 油 醇
Latex	*ru jiāo*	乳 胶

Medical Terms
Yī xué míng chēng
医 学 名 称

ECG	*xīn diàn tú*	心 电 图
EEG	*nǎo diàn tú*	脑 电 图
Nutrition	*yíng yǎng*	营 养
Intramuscular injection	*jī ròu zhù shè*	肌 肉 注 射
Intravenous injection	*jìng mài zhù shè*	静 脉 注 射
Abdominal laparotomy	*pōu fù jiǎn chá*	剖 腹 检 查
Sterilization	*jué yù*	绝 育

Physiotherapy	*wù lǐ liáo fǎ*	物 理 疗 法
Electrotherapy	*diàn liáo*	电 疗
Tuberculosis (T.B.)	*jié hé bìng*	结 核 病
Bronchitis	*zhī qì guǎn yán*	支 气 管 炎
Virosis	*bìng dú bìng*	病 毒 病
Coronary heart disease	*guàn xīn bìng*	冠 心 病
Cardiovascular disease	*xīn xué guǎn jí bìng*	心 血 管 疾 病
Hypertension	*gāo xuě yā*	高 血 压
Infectious disease	*chuán rǎn bìng (kong qi)*	传 染 病 (空 气)
Contagious disease	*chuán rǎn bìng (jie chu)*	传 染 病 (接 触)
Epidemic	*líu xíng bìng*	流 行 病
Chronic disease	*màn xìng jí bìng*	慢 性 疾 病
Ulcer	*kuì yáng*	溃 疡
Gastroenteritis	*wèi cháng yán*	胃 肠 炎
Appendicitis	*máng cháng yán*	盲 肠 炎
Diabetes	*táng niào bìng*	糖 尿 病

Arthritis	*fēng shī*	风 湿
Kidney stone	*shèn jié shí*	肾 结 石
Cancer	*ái*	癌
AIDS	*ài zī bìng*	艾 滋 病
Brain tumour	*nào zhǒng líu*	脑 肿 瘤
Miscarriage	*líu chǎn*	流 产
Measles	*má zhěn*	麻 疹
Chicken-pox	*shuǐ dòu*	水 痘
Small-pox	*tiān huā*	天 花
Polio	*xiǎo ér má bì zhèng*	小 儿 麻 痹 症
Malaria	*nuè jí*	疟 疾
Tetanus	*pò shāng fēng*	破 伤 风
Venereal Disease (VD)	*xìng bìng*	性 病
Fracture	*gu zhé*	骨 折
Tablet	*yào piàn*	药 片
Powder	*yào fěn*	药 粉
Mixture	*hé jì*	合 剂

Ointment	*ruǎn gāo*	软 膏
Balm	*qīng liáng yóu*	清 凉 油
Eye drops	*dī yǎn jì*	滴 眼 剂
Pain killer	*zhǐ téng jì*	止 疼 剂
Sleeping pill	*ān mián yào*	安 眠 药
Glucose	*pú táo táng*	葡 萄 糖
Vitamin	*wéi tā mìng*	维 他 命
Antibiotic	*kàng jūn sù*	抗 菌 素

Tools
Gōng jù
工 具

Axe	*fu zi*	斧 子
Hammer	*chuí zi*	锤 子
Anvil	*tiě zhēn*	铁 砧
Chisel	*zuó zi*	凿 子
Screw	*ló dīng*	螺 钉
Bolt	*ló mu*	螺 母
Die	*mó jù*	模 具

Wrench	*tái qián*	台 钳
Spanner	*bān shǒu*	扳 手
Screw driver	*ló sī dāo*	螺 丝 刀
Pincher	*qián zi*	钳 子
Nipper	*xiǎo jiā qián*	小 夹 钳
Nail	*tiě dīng*	铁 钉
Nail puller	*qǐ dīng qián*	起 钉 钳
Clip	*tú dīng*	图 钉
Forceps	*niè zi*	镊 子
Scissors	*jiǎn dāo*	剪 刀
Shear	*dà jiǎn dāo*	大 剪 刀
Driller	*zuàn tóu*	钻 头
Chuck	*zhā tóu*	轧 头
Cutter	*qiē gē jī*	切 割 机
Scraper	*guā xiāo dāo*	刮 削 刀
Slicer	*qiè piàn dāo*	切 片 刀
Ruler	*chǐ*	尺
Sprayer	*pèn wù qì*	喷 雾 器

Pump	*chōu shuǐ jī*	抽 水 机
Generator	*fā diàn jī*	发 电 机
Brush	*shuā zi*	刷 子

Computer Terms
Jì suàn jī shù yu
计 算 机 术 语

Hardware	*yìng jiàn*	硬 件
Software	*ruǎn jiàn*	软 件
Multimedia	*duō méi tǐ*	多 媒 体
Information Technology	*xìn xī jì shù*	信 息 技 术
Internet	*guó jì hù lián wǎng*	国 际 互 联 网
E-mail	*diàn zi yóu jiàn*	电 子 邮 件
Monitor	*xiǎn shì qì*	显 示 器
Hard disk	*yìng pán*	硬 盘
CPU	*zhōng yāng chù lǐ qì*	中 央 处 理 器

Pentium processor	*bēn téng xīn piàn*	奔 腾 芯 片
Memory	*nèi cún*	内 存
Sound card	*shēng kǎ*	声 卡
Keyboard	*jiàn pán*	键 盘
Mouse	*shu biāo*	鼠 标
Speaker	*yáng shēng qì*	杨 声 器
Microphone	*mài kè fēng*	麦 克 风
CD-ROM	*zhī dú guāng pán*	只 读 光 盘
Floppy	*cí pán*	磁 盘
Drive	*qū dòng qì*	驱 动 器
Modem	*tiáo zhì jiě tiáo qì*	调 制 解 调 器
Printer	*dǎ yìn jī*	打 印 机
Laser printer	*jī guāng dǎ yìn jī*	激 光 打 印 机
Scanner	*sǎo miáo yí*	扫 描 仪
DOS	*cí pán cāo zuò xì tǒng*	磁 盘 操 作 系 统
Windows	*shì chuāng*	视 窗

Graphics	*tú xíng*	图 形
Install	*zhuāng zài*	装 载
Download	*xià zài*	下 载
Database	*shù jù kù*	数 据 库
RAM	*suí jī cūn qǔ* *cūn chu qì*	随 机 存 取 存 储 器

APPENDIX

Family Relations
Qīn shu / qīn qí
亲 属 亲 戚

Wife	*qī zi*	妻 子
Husband	*zhàng fu*	丈 夫
Father	*fù qīn*	父 亲
Mother	*mu qīn*	母 亲
Elder Brother	*gē ge*	哥 哥
(his wife)	*sǎo sao*	嫂 嫂
Younger Brother	*dì di*	弟 弟
(his wife)	*dì mèi*	弟 妹
Elder Sister	*jiě jie*	姐 姐
(her husband)	*jiě fu*	姐 夫
Younger Sister	*mèi mei*	妹 妹
(her husband)	*mèi fu*	妹 夫
Son	*ér zi*	儿 子
Daugther-in-law	*ér xí*	儿 媳
Grand (son's) Son	*sūn zi*	孙 子

Grand (son's) Daughter	*sūn nǚ*	孙 女
Daughter	*nǚ ér*	女 儿
Son-in-law	*nǚ xù*	女 婿
Grand (daughter's)Son	*wài sūn*	外 孙
Grand (daughter's) Daughter	*wài sūn nǚ*	外 孙 女
Grand Father(maternal)	*wài zu fù*	外 祖 父
Grand Father(paternal)	*zu fù*	祖 父
Grand Mother(maternal)	*wài zú mu*	外 祖 母
Grand Mother(paternal)	*zú mu*	祖 母
Father's Elder Brother	*bó bo*	伯 伯
(his wife)	*bó mā*	伯 妈
Father's Younger Brother	*shū shu*	叔 叔
(his wife)	*shěn shen*	婶 婶
Father's Sister	*gū gu*	姑 姑
(her husband)	*gū fù*	姑 父
Mother's Sister	*yí*	姨
(her husband)	*yí fù*	姨 父
Mother's Brother	*jìu jiu*	舅 舅
(his wife)	*jìu mā*	舅 妈

Cousin Brother	*táng/biǎo xiōng*	堂/表 兄
Cousin Sister	*táng/biǎo jiě*	堂/表 姐
Mother-in-law	*jì mu*	继 母
Father-in-law	*jì fù*	继 父